Grammar Rules!

Tanya Gibb

Australian Curriculum Edition

Name: ______________________________

Class: ______________________________

Grammar Rules! Student Book 6
Australian Curriculum Edition
ISBN: 978 0 6550 9254 4

Designer and typesetter: Trish Hayes
Illustrator: Stephen Michael King
Series editor: Marie James
Indigenous consultant: Al Fricker

Acknowledgement of Country
Matilda Education Australia acknowledges all Aboriginal and Torres Strait Islander Traditional Custodians of Country and recognises their continuing connection to land, sea, culture, and community. We pay our respects to Elders past and present.

This edition published in 2024 by **Matilda Education Australia**, an imprint of Meanwhile Education Pty
PO Box 118, Burwood, Victoria, Australia 3125
T: 1300 277 235
E: customersupport@matildaed.com.au
W: www.matildaeducation.com.au

First edition published in 2008 by Macmillan Science and Education Australia Pty Ltd

Publication data
Author: Tanya Gibb
Title: *Grammar Rules! Student Book 6 Australian Curriculum Edition*
ISBN: 978 0 6550 9254 4

A catalogue record for this book is available from the National Library of Australia

Printed in China by Central
Jun-2025

CONTENTS

NOTE TO TEACHERS AND PARENTS

Grammar Rules!

Grammar Rules! comprehensively addresses the interrelated strands of Language, Literature and Literacy in the **Australian Curriculum English V9**, 2022. The *Grammar Rules!* series supports students' development of knowledge, understanding and skills in reading, viewing, speaking, writing and creating texts.

The **Australian Curriculum English** recognises that learning in English is recursive and cumulative, so each book in the *Grammar Rules!* series is designed to build on concepts covered previously and for an expanding range of audiences and purposes.

Grammar Rules! provides a conceptually sound scope and sequence of context-based activities that support teaching and learning in English. Although the title for the series is *Grammar Rules!*, the series in not just about grammar. The series provides opportunities for students to explore texts created for aesthetic, imaginative, reflective, informative, persuasive, analytical or critical purposes, or any combination of these, as well as learn how to create texts for different audiences.

The model texts provided in the workbooks can be used for reading comprehension and for learning about text structures and features as well as for vocabulary expansion. *Student Book 6* also teaches the conventions of punctuation and some aspects of spelling, for example, word roots (etymology); literary elements, such as onomatopoeia, metaphor, simile, personification, imagery and alliteration; the way visual elements function to support or construct meaning, as well as features such as character, setting and plot in narrative texts, and narrative structures, including chronological order and flashback.

Grammar Rules! comprehensively supports the aim of the **Australian Curriculum English V9** to 'help students learn to analyse, understand, communicate and build relationships with others and the world around them. It helps create confident communicators, imaginative and critical thinkers, and informed citizens.'

Student Book 6

Units of work

Student Book 6 contains 35 weekly units of work presented in a conceptually sound scope and sequence. The intention is for students to work through the units in the sequence in which they are presented. See the **Scope and Sequence Chart** on pages 6–7 for more information. There are regular Revision Units that can be used for consolidation or assessment purposes.

The sample texts in *Student Book 6* are generally based on the themes of places, times and cultures. This allows teachers and students to focus on the way language is structured in the different types of texts according to purpose and audience. Students can then use this knowledge to critically evaluate, respond to and create texts in other learning areas.

Icons

Encourages students to create texts of their own to demonstrate their understanding of the text structures and features taught in the unit. These activities focus on written language; however, many also provide opportunities for using spoken language to engage with others, make presentations and develop skills in using ICT.

Highlights useful grammatical rules and concepts. The rule is always introduced the first time students need it to complete an activity.

Tells students that a special hint is provided for an activity. It might be a tip about language features or a reminder to look at a rule in a previous unit.

Grammar Rules! Glossary

A valuable glossary is provided at the end of *Student Book 6*. Teachers and students can use this as a reference for terminology and rules introduced in *Student Book 6*. Page references are also given for the point in the book where the rule or tip was first introduced so that students can go back to that unit if they need more information or further revision of the concept.

Pull-Out Writing Log

At the centre of *Student Book 6* is a practical pull-out Writing Log so that students can keep track of the texts they have created or attempted to create. The Writing Log also includes a handy reminder of the writing process, as well as a checklist of types of texts for students to try.

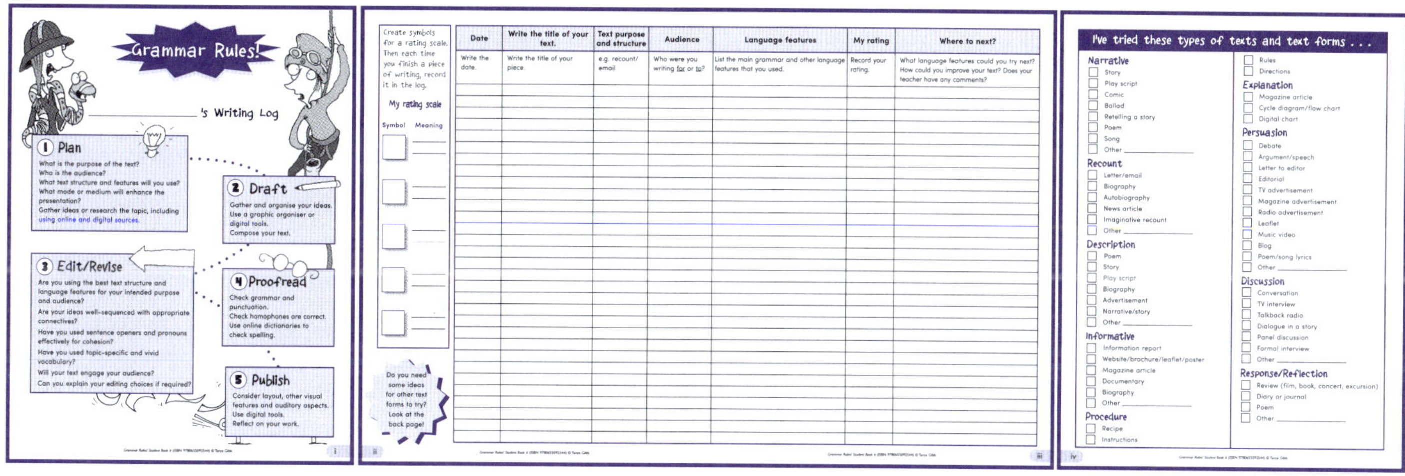

Unit At A Glance

Unit tag
States the main language focus

Text sample
Provides a context for learning about language

Sequenced activities
Activities focus on reading comprehension, text features and structures, vocabulary, grammar or punctuation

Tip!
Reminds or gives a special hint

Type of text
Highlights the type of text and purpose of the sample text

Try it yourself!
Gives students opportunities to apply their knowledge and skills to create their own texts. Students can engage in planning, drafting and editing their texts and using different modes and media to enhance presentation of their texts.

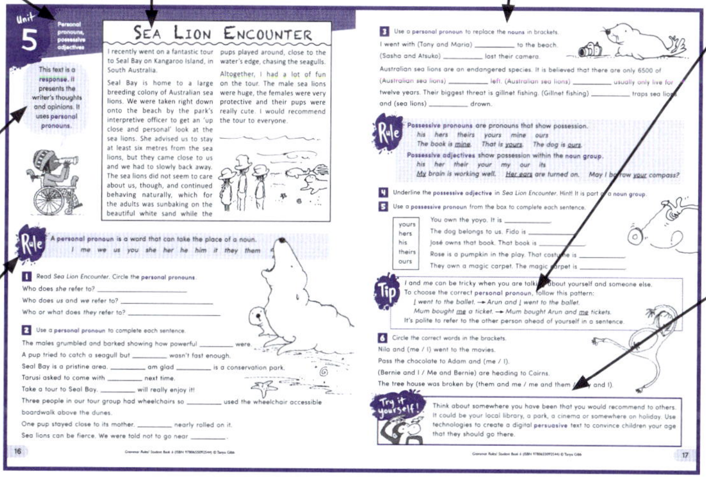

Rule!
Introduces students to a new concept

Grammar Rules! Teacher Resource Book 3–6

Full teacher support for *Student Book 6* is provided by *Grammar Rules! Teacher Resource Book 3–6*.

Here you will find valuable background information about teaching English along with practical resources, such as:

- strategies for teaching text structures and features
- literacy games and activities
- assessment strategies
- grammar and punctuation wall charts
- teaching tips for every unit in *Student Book 6*
- answers for every unit in *Student Book 6*.

Scope and Sequence

This scope and sequence chart is based on the requirements of the Australian Curriculum English.

Unit	Unit name Type of text	Purpose of text	Clauses, sentences	Nouns, noun groups, pronouns, adjectives	Verbs and verb groups	Adverbs, prepositional phrases, connectives, conjunctions	Language and vocabulary	Literary devices
1	**Dear Grandma and Grandpa** Email	to respond to inform			verb groups, tenses, auxiliary verbs	adverbs, conjunctions		
2	**Green Sea Turtles of the Great Barrier Reef** Report	to inform to describe		noun groups, adjectival phrases			objective and subjective language	simile
3	**A Trip to the Zoo** Personal recount	to inform to respond	compound and complex sentences			adverbs, conjunctions		
4	**The Monster in the Labyrinth** Narrative – myth	to retell a myth		adjectives		prepositional phrases	paragraphs, antonyms	similes
5	**Sea Lion Encounter** Personal recount	to respond to inform	sentences	pronouns, possessive adjectives				
6	REVISION							
7	**A Conversation** Poem	to entertain to describe		abstract nouns				proverbs, idiom, narrator
8	**My Journal** Personal reflection	to reflect to respond		noun groups, determiners, adjectives				
9	**The 'Most Famous' Famous Landmark** Discussion	to consider alternative viewpoints, to give an opinion	sentences		verb groups, modal verbs, tense		quoted speech, paragraphs	
10	**Sydney Shows Off** News article	to entertain to inform	sentences				emotive vocabulary, reported speech, synonyms	
11	**Greetings from the North-West** Postcard	to inform to entertain					informal language, contractions	imagery
12	REVISION							
13	**The Deadly Mosquito** Information report and instructions	to inform to instruct	clauses, sentence openers, reference	noun groups	verbs		cohesion, reference	
14	**Curse of the Pharaohs** Narrative	to entertain	clauses, sentences	pronouns		connectives		
15	**Travel Tips** Leaflet/brochure	to inform to instruct	complex sentences, adjectival and adverbial clauses		relating verbs	connectives		
16	**Come to China!** Advertisement	to persuade			modal verbs	modal adverbs	emotive vocabulary	
17	**Uluru** Response	to inform to describe	complex sentences, clauses			prepositional phrases		imagery
18	REVISION							

Grammar Rules! Student Book 6 (ISBN 9780655092544) © Tanya Gibb

Unit	Unit name Type of text	Purpose of text	Clauses, sentences	Nouns, noun groups, pronouns, adjectives	Verbs and verb groups	Adverbs, prepositional phrases, connectives, conjunctions	Language and vocabulary	Literary devices
19	**Where Would You Go?** Argument	to persuade	sentences	possessive apostrophes, collective nouns			objective and subjective language, cohesion	
20	**Land Sale!** Advertisement							alliteration, parody, fractured tales
21	**A Future** Poem	to respond to reflect		articles, noun groups			cohesion, word associations	
22	**Mummification** Explanation	to inform	sentences	possessive apostrophes		connectives	time sequence, punctuation, comic strips	
23	**The Accidental Traveller** Narrative	to entertain	sentences	first- and third- person pronouns				flashback, idiom, narrative voice
24	REVISION							
25	**Correspondence** Email	to inform	open and closed questions				degrees of formality	
26	**The Melting Pot** Menu	to inform to persuade		noun groups	verb groups		word associations	alliteration, metaphor
27	**The Rights of the Child** Podcast	to inform to persuade			verb groups, subject-verb agreement		emotive vocabulary, acronyms	proverbs
28	**Top Wonder** Written argument	to argue a point of view, to persuade			verb groups		subjective language, paragraphs	
29	**Resistance** Report	to inform to persuade	clauses (dependent, main, embedded)		verb groups		emotive vocabulary, subjective language	
30	REVISION							
31	**Chichén Itzá** Media interview	to inform to describe to persuade		pronouns, noun groups			reference	
32	**Lion Safari, Kenya** Advertisement	to persuade		nouns, noun groups	verbs		homophones, prefixes	personification, imagery
33	**Don't Let Them In** Narrative and playscript	to entertain					dialogue, point of view	character, plot, narrative voice, flashback
34	**Multicultural Australia** Information text/ Report	to inform		noun groups			word origins, affixes, brackets	
35	REVISION							

Unit 1

Verb groups, tense, adverbs, conjunctions

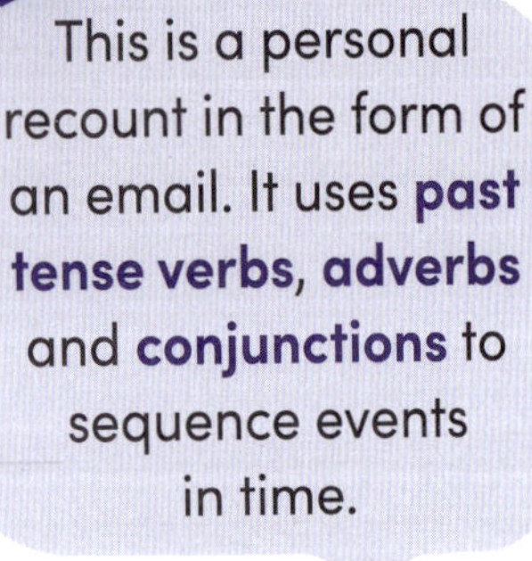

This is a personal recount in the form of an email. It uses **past tense verbs**, **adverbs** and **conjunctions** to sequence events in time.

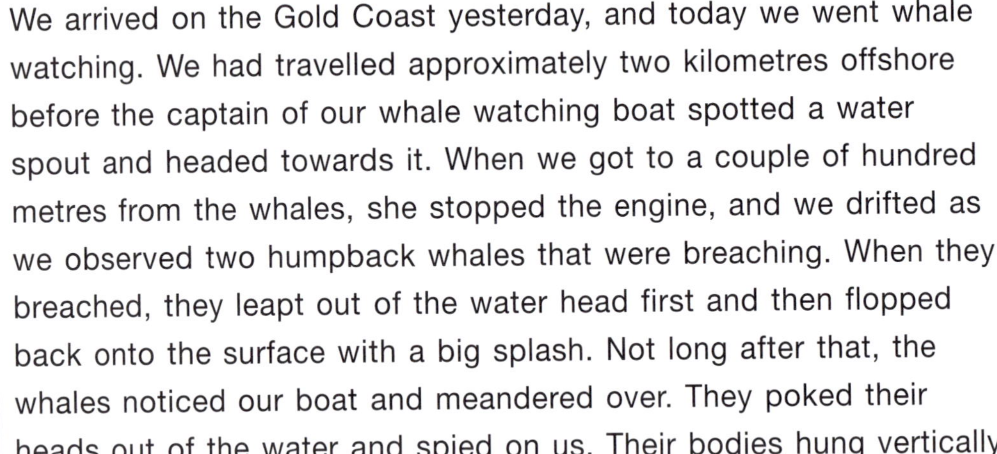

Dear Grandma and Grandpa,

We arrived on the Gold Coast yesterday, and today we went whale watching. We had travelled approximately two kilometres offshore before the captain of our whale watching boat spotted a water spout and headed towards it. When we got to a couple of hundred metres from the whales, she stopped the engine, and we drifted as we observed two humpback whales that were breaching. When they breached, they leapt out of the water head first and then flopped back onto the surface with a big splash. Not long after that, the whales noticed our boat and meandered over. They poked their heads out of the water and spied on us. Their bodies hung vertically in the water. They were magnificent.

I loved today. I love you.

Kenan

Rule **Verbs** and **verb groups** are words for doing (action), saying, thinking and relating (being).

have made *will be* *was thinking* *did speak* *had finished*

1 Read *Dear Grandma and Grandpa.* Underline the **verbs** and **verb groups**.

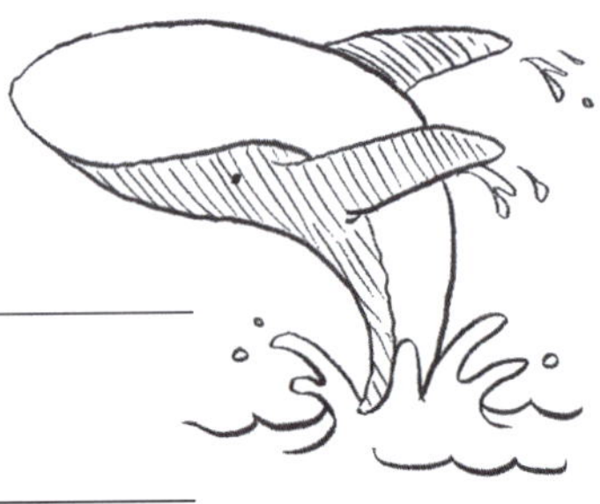

Write three **verbs** or **verb groups** that tell what the humans did.

______________ ______________ ______________

Write three **verbs** or **verb groups** that tell what the whales did.

______________ ______________ ______________

Rule The form of a **verb** shows whether an activity happened in the past, is happening now, happens regularly or is always happening, or might happen in the future. This is called **tense**.

Auxiliary verbs (*did, have, was*) and **suffixes** (*–ed, –t, –ing*) help to show the **tense**.

past tense	*I kissed*	*I did kiss*	*I have kissed*	*I was kissing*
present tense	*I am kissing*	*We kiss*	**future tense**	*I will kiss*

2 Write **verbs** with two different **suffixes** from *Dear Grandma and Grandpa* that show **past tense**.

______________ ______________

3 Write **verb groups** with two different **auxiliary verbs** from *Dear Grandma and Grandpa* that show **past tense**.

______________ ______________

4 Write the **thinking verb** that tells how Kenan felt about whale watching. ______________

Grammar Rules! Student Book 6 (ISBN 9780655092544) © Tanya Gibb

5 Change the form of each **verb** to show that the action happened in the **past**.

The tour guide (will advise) _______________ us about whale behaviours.

The captain (announces) _______________, 'Jingeri jimbelung, hello friends.'

We (can attract) _______________ the whales' attention.

The whales (swim) _______________ here from Antarctica.

I (am enjoying) _______________ the whale watching tour.

6 Complete each sentence with an **auxiliary verb** to show that the actions happened in the **past**.

was
have
were
did
have

I _____________ thought about visiting my aunt.

The whales _____________ travelled a long way.

We _____________ busy on our holiday in Kombumerri country.

I _____________ taught some words in the Yugambeh language.

The Kombumerri people _____________ not have a didgeridoo as a traditional instrument.

Rule

Adverbs can help establish a time frame for what is happening in a text.

yesterday soon now tomorrow finally immediately weekly

Conjunctions can link clauses in a sentence to show the time sequence.

when then while until since before

7 Write the words in *Dear Grandma and Grandpa* that show time sequence.

____

8 Use a **conjunction** from the box to complete each sentence. Use a capital letter to start a sentence.

after
when
since
when

I love whales more than ever __________ I went to the Gold Coast.

__________ I saw the humpbacks, I felt really happy.

__________ we were on holiday, we stayed at a caravan park at the beach.

__________ we ate dinner, we went for a walk.

9 Use an **adverb** from the box to complete each sentence.

now
soon
later
finally
yesterday

I hurt my foot ____________________.

I have English homework _____________ but I can practise my guitar _____________.

Dinner will be ready _____________.

Arianna _______________ finished her homework.

Try it yourself!

Write a **personal recount** that tells about somewhere you have been or something you have done. Or, write a recount from the **point of view** of a character in a novel you are reading telling about somewhere that character has been. Use **adverbs** and **conjunctions** to sequence events in time. Publish the recount as an email to a family member or friend, or to the story character's family member or friend.

Unit 2

Noun groups, simile, objective and subjective language

This informative text is a **description**. It uses **noun groups** with **descriptive** and **classifying adjectives** to describe the subject.

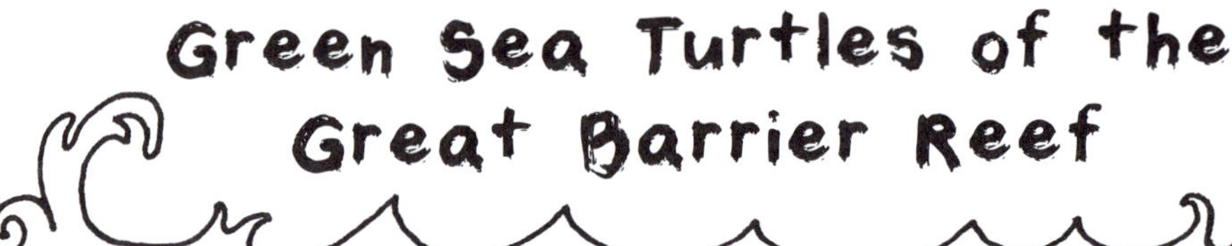

The Great Barrier Reef is a magnificent habitat and nesting area for the critically endangered green turtle. The adult green turtles love to eat the tasty seaweed and algae found in the warm waters of the Pacific Ocean. These gentle plant eaters are olive green in colour with perhaps some brown, reddish-brown or black markings. Each turtle has quite distinctive face markings. The shell is a cross between circular and heart-shaped and might grow to a metre long. It is a creamy colour underneath. Green turtles have oar-shaped flippers to pull themselves through the water like a canoe, and their heads and nostrils make them look like little aliens when they rise above the surface of their watery tropical paradise.

Rule

Noun groups can be expanded to give a detailed description of a person, place, animal or thing. A noun group can include an **article**, **descriptive adjectives** and another noun used as an adjective to **classify**. *a gooey chocolate brownie*

An **adjectival phrase** usually follows directly after the **noun** it is describing. *a thin and crispy pizza with cheese and mushrooms*

1 Read *Green Sea Turtles of the Great Barrier Reef.*

Write four **noun groups** that include **descriptive adjectives**.

____

____

____

____

2 Create your own **noun groups** by completing the table.

Descriptive adjective	Noun used to classify	Noun
magnificent	coral	reef
		dog
decrepit		
	guitar	
	truck	

Grammar Rules! Student Book 6 (ISBN 9780655092544) © Tanya Gibb

3 Build interesting **noun groups** for the noun *ocean*. Use any combination of **adjectives**.

_______________________________ ocean

_______________________________ ocean

_______________________________ ocean

_______________________________ ocean

Rule!

Language can be **objective** (factual) or **subjective** (evaluative).

objective: *Green turtles eat seaweed and algae.*

subjective: *Green turtles love to eat seaweed and algae.*

4 Write two examples of **subjective** language from the text.

____

____

Rule!

A **simile** is a literary device. It builds an image of a noun by comparing it to something else using 'like' or 'as'.

She ran as fast as lightning. Its eyes were like black marbles.

5 Find two **similes** in *Green Sea Turtles of the Great Barrier Reef*. What two things are compared in each simile?

____

____

6 Draw lines linking the word groups to create **similes**.

as dry as	cats and dogs
as cold as	a bone
fight like	thunder
work like	ice
sings like	an angel
a face like	a dog

7 Create **similes** of your own.

as hungry as _______________

as sparkly as _______________

snores like a _______________

sings like a _______________

eats like a _______________

as slow as _______________

Write a **description** of a real or imaginary place. Use interesting **noun groups** to create a detailed description. Use **similes** to add to the imagery.

Unit 3

Sentences, adverbs

My Trip to the Zoo

Last Saturday, my cousin, Satoshi, and I went to the zoo.

We visited the apes first. My favourite apes are orangutans because they are very clever. We watched one orangutan. He gathered a pile of empty potato sacks, and he carefully stacked them into a pile. He fussed with the sacks and finally sat on them. He was extremely industrious.

After the apes, we visited the bears and the elephants but we decided that our favourite animals for the day were the mountain goats. They nimbly climbed their rock mountain, even the babies.

Overall, I enjoyed the day very much. It was totally amazing, and I hope to go back there soon.

This personal recount uses a variety of sentence types to retell and evaluate events.

Rule

A **clause** is a group of words that expresses an idea and contains a **verb**.
A **simple sentence** is a single clause.
A **compound sentence** consists of **independent clauses** that each make sense on their own. A **complex sentence** consists of two or more linked clauses where one clause is the **main (independent) clause** and the other clauses are **dependent** on it to make sense.

1 Read *My Trip to the Zoo*. Circle the **verbs** and **verb groups**. Underline the **conjunctions** *(and, because, but)*.

2 Form **compound sentences**. Join each pair of **simple sentences** using a **conjunction** from the box.

and	but	yet	or

The meerkats were cute. The otters were cuter than the meerkats.

____

We liked the lemurs. We liked the sun bears.

____

It wasn't very crowded. We couldn't find seats together.

____

We could watch the 'Birds of Flight' at 1 pm. We could see the crocodiles at 1 pm.

____

3 Add an **independent clause** to each line to create **compound sentences**.

We had lasagne for dinner and ________________________________.

The beach was crowded but ________________________________.

I could read a science fiction novel or ________________________________.

I prefer science fiction so ________________________________.

Rule

Adverbs can tell manner (*quietly*), time (*soon*) or place (*there*).
Adverbs can add meaning to verbs.
smiled cheekily *danced happily* *cackled madly*
Adverbs can add meaning to adjectives.
extremely talented *really witty* *very honest*

4 Underline the **adverb** and circle the **verb** in each sentence.

The lions roared loudly.

The koalas dozed peacefully.

The bears looked at us occasionally.

Long, blue giraffe tongues poked out stickily.

5 Underline the **adverb** and circle the **adjective** in each sentence.

The bears looked very relaxed.

The whole thing was totally terrifying.

Zoos are extremely interesting places.

The goats were really clever.

6 Re-read *My Trip to the Zoo*.

Find three **adverbs** that add meaning to **verbs**.

____

Find three **adverbs** that add meaning to **adjectives**.

____

7 Write a sentence starting with each **adverb** below.

Needlessly ________________________________

Carelessly ________________________________

Wearily ________________________________

Bravely ________________________________

Quickly ________________________________

Choose an animal described in *My Trip to the Zoo*. Write about the events from the animal's **point of view**. Describe the animal's thoughts and feelings and what the animal is seeing and hearing. Use detailed **noun groups** and **adverbs**.

Unit 4

Prepositional phrases, adjectives, similes, antonyms

This imaginative text is a **narrative** that tells part of a Greek myth. It uses **prepositional phrases** and **adjectives** to set the scene.

The Monster in the Labyrinth

In a dark, cavernous underground labyrinth, beneath the city of Knossos, on the island of Crete, lurked a dreadful beast. The beast was a Minotaur. It had the body of a man, the head of a bull and it feasted on human flesh. Its horns were as sharp as swords. Its bloodcurdling bellow sent terror into the hearts of all who heard it. The labyrinth was a gigantic, winding maze, and once a person entered, they were never seen again. At the beginning of every year, to placate the beast, King Minos sent seven young men and seven young women into the maze as sacrifices to the Minotaur.

1 Read *The Monster in the Labyrinth*. What happened to people sent into the labyrinth?

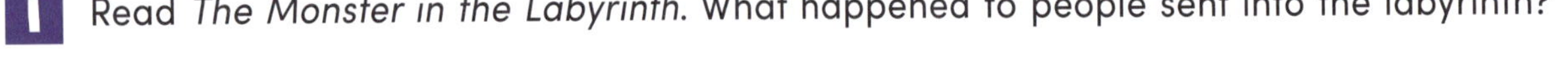

Rule

A **prepositional phrase** consists of a **preposition** (e.g. *in, on, under, between, with, for, by*) followed by a **noun** or **pronoun**. A phrase can tell place, time or manner.

across the bridge   *by morning*   *for a long time*   *with its claws*   *without him*

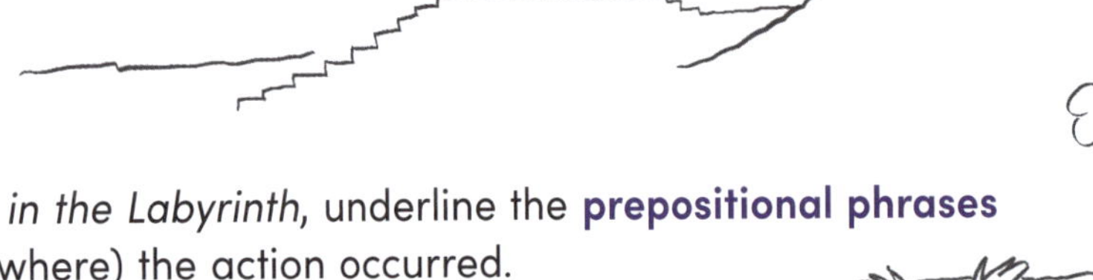

2 In *The Monster in the Labyrinth*, underline the **prepositional phrases** that tell place (where) the action occurred.

3 Write the **prepositional phrase** in *The Monster in the Labyrinth* that tells time (when the action occurred).

4 Add three **prepositional phrases** to the beginning of this sentence to set the scene and tell where.

______________________________ lurked a ferocious dinosaur.

5 The writer of *The Monster in the Labyrinth* has forgotten to use paragraphs. Talk with a partner. Draw a / where each new paragraph should start.

Grammar Rules! Student Book 6 (ISBN 9780655092544) ©Tanya Gibb

6 Write the **simile** used in *The Monster in the Labyrinth.*

Tip: Remember the rule on page 11.

___

What does the use of this **simile** add to the myth? ___

___

7 Create **similes** of your own to suit the minotaur myth.

The maze was as ___.

The Minotaur's head was as ___.

The Minotaur's bellow was like ___.

Rule Some **adjectives** tell the quantity or order of a noun.
one mango the last mango the second row a few cherries many guests

8 Find one **number adjective** used in *The Monster in the Labyrinth.* ___

9 Choose a **number adjective** from the box to complete each sentence.

dozen many last each thirty every some

He tried hard but still came ___ in the race.

Our school has planted ___ eucalypts.

___ children walk to school ___ day.

I'll need a ___ eggs for the omelette.

___ child can have a turn.

___ people are diligent recyclers.

10 Find six **descriptive adjectives** used in *The Monster in the Labyrinth.*

___

Which of the adjectives do you think adds the best description to the story? Why?

___

11 Find two **noun groups** in *The Monster in the Labyrinth* that use a noun to classify in a noun group.

___ ___

12 Find **antonyms** in *The Monster in the Labyrinth* for 'delightful' and 'straight'.

___ ___

Rule **Antonyms** are words with opposite meanings.
pleased → displeased
fight → surrender

Try it yourself! Research the ending of the myth *Theseus and the Minotaur* and draw a comic strip to represent the events in the **narrative**. Or, research another myth from around the world and prepare a retelling to present to your class. You might like to choose a First Nations' Dreaming story to retell.

Unit 5

Personal pronouns, possessive adjectives

This text is a **response**. It presents the writer's thoughts and opinions. It uses **personal pronouns**.

Sea Lion Encounter

I recently went on a fantastic tour to Seal Bay on Kangaroo Island, in South Australia.

Seal Bay is home to a large breeding colony of Australian sea lions. We were taken right down onto the beach by the park's interpretive officer to get an 'up close and personal' look at the sea lions. She advised us to stay at least six metres from the sea lions, but they came close to us and we had to slowly back away. The sea lions did not seem to care about us, though, and continued behaving naturally, which for the adults was sunbaking on the beautiful white sand while the pups played around, close to the water's edge, chasing the seagulls.

Altogether, I had a lot of fun on the tour. The male sea lions were huge, the females were very protective and their pups were really cute. I would recommend the tour to everyone.

Rule A **personal pronoun** is a word that can take the place of a noun.

I me we us you she her he him it they them

1 Read *Sea Lion Encounter*. Circle the **personal pronouns**.

Who does *she* refer to? ______________________

Who does *us* and *we* refer to? ______________________

Who or what does *they* refer to? ______________________

2 Use a **personal pronoun** to complete each sentence.

The males grumbled and barked showing how powerful ________ were.

A pup tried to catch a seagull but ________ wasn't fast enough.

Seal Bay is a pristine area. ________ am glad ________ is a conservation park.

Tarusi asked to come with ________ next time.

Take a tour to Seal Bay. ________ will really enjoy it!

Three people in our tour group had wheelchairs so ________ used the wheelchair accessible boardwalk above the dunes.

One pup stayed close to its mother. ________ nearly rolled on it.

Sea lions can be fierce. We were told not to go near ________.

Grammar Rules! Student Book 6 (ISBN 9780655092544) © Tanya Gibb

3 Use a **personal pronoun** to replace the **nouns** in brackets.

I went with (Tony and Maria) ___________ to the beach.

(Sasha and Atsuko) ___________ lost their camera.

Australian sea lions are an endangered species. It is believed that there are only 6500 of (Australian sea lions) ___________ left. (Australian sea lions) ___________ usually only live for twelve years. Their biggest threat is gillnet fishing. (Gillnet fishing) ___________ traps sea lions and (sea lions) ___________ drown.

Rule

Possessive pronouns are pronouns that show possession.

his hers theirs yours mine ours

The book is mine. That is yours. The dog is ours.

Possessive adjectives show possession within the **noun group**.

his her their your my our its

My brain is working well. Her ears are turned on. May I borrow your compass?

4 Underline the **possessive adjective** in *Sea Lion Encounter*. Hint! It is part of a **noun group**.

5 Use a **possessive pronoun** from the box to complete each sentence.

yours hers his theirs ours

You own the yoyo. It is ___________.

The dog belongs to us. Fido is ___________.

José owns that book. That book is ___________.

Rose is a pumpkin in the play. That costume is ___________.

They own a magic carpet. The magic carpet is ___________.

Tip

I and *me* can be tricky when you are talking about yourself and someone else.
To choose the correct **personal pronoun**, follow this pattern:

I went to the ballet. → Arun and I went to the ballet.

Mum bought me a ticket. → Mum bought Arun and me tickets.

It's polite to refer to the other person ahead of yourself in a sentence.

6 Circle the correct words in the brackets.

Nila and (me / I) went to the movies.

Pass the chocolate to Adam and (me / I).

(Bernie and I / Me and Bernie) are heading to Cairns.

The tree house was broken by (them and me / me and them / they and I).

Try it yourself!

Think about somewhere you have been that you would recommend to others. It could be your local library, a park, a cinema or somewhere on holiday. Use technologies to create a digital **persuasive** text to convince children your age that they should go there.

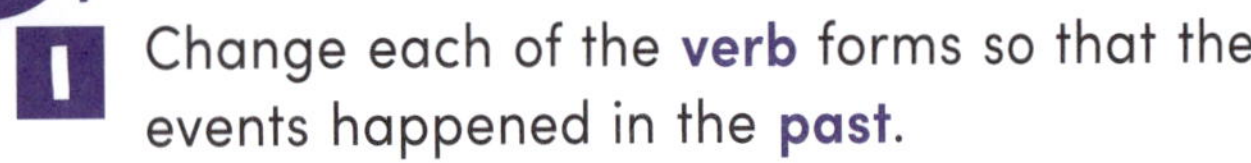

Unit 6 Revision

1 Change each of the **verb** forms so that the events happened in the **past**.

My friends (eat) ______________ yum cha.

We (swim) ______________ between the flags.

We (drink) ______________ tomato juice.

The postie (brings) ______________ our mail.

I (enjoy) ______________ the show.

2 Circle the **auxiliary verb** in each sentence.

I have eaten too many pineapples.

I did enjoy the concert.

My marks will improve if I study.

I do like ice-skating.

I was advised about the new rules.

3 Use an adverb or phrase from the box on each line to show the time sequence for events.

finally	of the year	soon	for ages	in July

It is ______________ NAIDOC Week and the NAIDOC Awards will be announced ______________. I have been waiting ______________ to hear the winner of the 'Caring for Country and Culture' Award. NAIDOC Week is held ______________. It is my favourite week ______________ because there are lots of activities and celebrations.

4 What do the pronouns *It/it* and *him* refer to in the text below?

Woofy has a favourite chew toy. It is shaped like a pickle. I gave it to him.

____

5 Rewrite the sentences using **past tense verbs**.

My dear old Aunt Amy loves pickles. She even eats pickles for breakfast.

____

6 Complete the table to create interesting **noun groups**.

Number adjective	Descriptive adjective	Classifier	Noun
		horse	
two			
	hideous		
		motor	
	spectacular		
some		timber	

Grammar Rules! Student Book 6 (ISBN 9780655092544) © Tanya Gibb

7 Create a **simile** of your own for each of the following.

as boring as ____________________

as quiet as ____________________

laughs like a ____________________

8 Use a **conjunction** from the box to join each pair of clauses. Write the new sentences.

and	but	so	or	because

My brother is performing at the NAIDOC concert. We'll need to arrive early.

____

There will be cultural activities. There will be food stalls.

____

Parking is difficult. There's a free bus service.

____

We might drive. We might use the free shuttle bus.

____

My family loves the art exhibition. The art works celebrate culture and country.

____

9 Complete each sentence with an **adverb** that tells manner (how).

The robot beeped ____________________.

The octopus swam ____________________ away from the whale.

Our friends were ____________________ excited.

The numbats were ____________________ defenceless.

Beep!

10 Write three **prepositional phrases** that tell where to set the scene for a scary story.

____

____________________ skulked the vile villain.

11 Use a **pronoun** from the box to complete each sentence.

they them yours hers

I went with (Mum and Dad) ____________ to the library.

(Juanita and Jeff) ____________ won tenpin bowling.

You own the car. The responsibility for it is ____________.

My sister sings a lot. The microphone is ____________.

12 Circle the correct words in the brackets.

Pass the papers to (Iris and me / Iris and I).

(We / us) senior students need our own common room.

(Boris and I / Me and Boris) will drive to Broken Hill, Wilyakali Lands, tomorrow.

Unit 7

Proverbs, idiom, narrator, abstract nouns

The narrator of the poem uses **proverbs** and **idiom** to illustrate their relationship with their grandmother.

A Conversation

I heard it on the grapevine, she said.
You're saving for a bike.
That'll cost you an arm and a leg.
I'm doing extra jobs, I said.
You can wash my car
she said
but don't cut any corners.
Piece of cake, I said.
It's not rocket science
but no need to pay me.
So I washed the car
and when I was done
she gave me $10 anyway
but she said,
Don't give up your day job.

Nan doesn't beat around the bush.
She's as sharp as a tack.
She values hard work
and she's frugal with her cash.
Time is money
and waste not want not, she chants.
I take Nan with a grain of salt.
She's a real leg puller.
She's also the whole nine yards
and the best thing since sliced bread
whenever you need grand-mothering.
She's loyal and loving
through thick and thin
and on that we see eye to eye.

By Tanya Dalgleish©

1 Underline the **simile** in the poem. What does it mean?

____

Rule

A **proverb** is a well-known saying or expression that offers wisdom or advice.

Actions speak louder than words. It's better to be safe than sorry.

An **idiom** is an expression that has an understood meaning that is not the same as the meaning of the individual words.

He's sitting on the fence (meaning 'undecided').

2 What does each expression below mean? Ask family members and other adults or use the internet.

Heard it on the grapevine _______________________

Costs an arm and a leg _______________________

Don't cut any corners. _______________________

Not rocket science _______________________

Don't give up your day job. _______________________

Don't beat around the bush. _______________________

Waste not want not. _______________________

Take it with a grain of salt. _______________________

The best thing since sliced bread _______________________

See eye to eye _______________________

Grammar Rules! Student Book 6 (ISBN 9780655092544) © Tanya Gibb

3 Describe the relationship between the **narrator** (the person recounting events in the poem) and the grandmother. ______________________________

____

How do you know? ______________________________

4 What does the narrator mean in describing the grandmother as *loyal and loving through thick and thin?*

____

In what circumstances might a grandmother need to demonstrate this kind of loyalty?

____

5 Identify a **compound sentence** in the poem. Write it on the lines. ______________________________

____

6 What is the meaning of *frugal*? ______________________________

Rule

Abstract nouns represent things that cannot be seen or touched. Adding, removing or changing a **suffix** can change a noun into an **adjective**.

fear → fearful *loyalty → loyal* *friend → friendly* *anger → angry*

7 Add, remove or change the **suffixes** to form an **adjective** from each abstract noun.

hunger ______	danger ______	mischief ______
capability ______	energy ______	destruction ______
health ______	offence ______	belief ______
hatred ______	acceptance ______	beauty ______

8 Use **conjunctions** of your choice to link the clauses and create complex sentences.

I'm doing extra jobs. I'm saving money for a bike. I'll do whatever jobs you can give me.

____

I can wash cars. I can walk dogs. I can pull weeds from a garden. I'm willing to work hard. I'm saving money for a new bike.

____

____

9 Write four **adjectives** of your own to describe the grandmother in *A Conversation*.

____

Try it yourself!

Write a poem that shows the relationship between two people. You might base your poem on *A Conversation* and write the poem in the first person using **personal pronouns** and **reported speech**. Publish and perform your poem.

Unit 8

Determiners, adjectives, noun groups

My Journal

Many people come to live in Australia from places all over the world. Sometimes their countries have been involved in wars or natural disasters. Sometimes people are persecuted in their countries of birth for reasons of religion, race or politics. Some become immigrants. Some are refugees or asylum seekers.

I think the most important thing all those people want is a better life. It could be an incredible adventure to move to a new country. But it must be very scary to leave behind everything you know and start again somewhere new and strange, especially if you are forced to leave loved ones and all your possessions behind. I wonder how I would cope in a different country, in a new home, learning a new language, at a new school, my whole life turned upside down. I'd be really scared.

In this text, the writer reflects on a topic and makes use of varied **noun groups** with **determiners** and **adjectives** to express a personal response.

Rule

Determiners (including **articles**) are used in a noun group to identify or point out.

that this those these the a an

Articles can be definite (*the*) or indefinite (*a, an*).

1 Read *My Journal*. Find and write a **noun group** that:

has a **determiner** ______________________

has a **possessive adjective** ______________________

includes an **adjective** for **number** or **quantity** ______________________

includes a **descriptive adjective** ______________________

Tip Remember the rule on page 10.

2 Complete each sentence with a **determiner**. Use each determiner once.

This
That
These
An
A
The

__________ crocodile swam in my pool.

__________ igloo is designed to keep out the cold.

__________ car is filthy.

__________ onions are delicious.

__________ bus to Devonport is late.

__________ guinea pig is biting my sock.

3 Write definitions for the following terms in *My Journal*. Use a dictionary.

immigrant ______________________

asylum seeker ______________________

refugee ______________________

Grammar Rules! Student Book 6 (ISBN 9780655092544) © Tanya Gibb

4 Complete each **noun group** with a **possessive adjective** from the box. Use one of the words three times. Use a capital letter if the word begins a sentence.

her
their
my

Halyna's family was forced to leave ________ home in Ukraine. Halyna joined ________ class. I have helped her to improve ________ English. ________ class has made her welcome. I was born in Finland but Australia is now ________ home, too.

By Peta

Rule **Adjectives** used to compare or show a preference have **comparative** and **superlative** forms. Adjectives with more than two syllables usually compare by using 'more' or 'most'.

	adjective	**comparative**	**superlative**
regular	*pretty*	*prettier*	*prettiest*
irregular	*bad*	*worse*	*worst*
2+ syllables	*successful*	*more successful*	*most successful*

5 Write a **noun group** from *My Journal* that includes an **adjective** that compares. ________________

6 Complete the table. Write the **adjective** forms that compare.

Adjective	**Comparative**	**Superlative**
frightening		
strange		
scary		
lucky		
good		

7 Use the correct form of the **adjective** in brackets to complete each sentence.

The yellow daffodils were (pretty) ________________ than the irises.

I was (worried) ________________ about moving house than Marcel.

Billy was the (fast) ________________ climber of all the goats.

I was the (please) ________________ of everyone.

Tip **Absolute adjectives** are adjectives that do not have a comparative or superlative form.
dead: You can't be *deader, deadest, more dead* or *most dead* – only *dead.*

dead *empty* *full* *alive* *perfect* *right* *wrong*

8 Find the **absolute adjective** in *My Journal.* ________________

Try it yourself! Think about a time when you have been in a new situation. It might be a new school, a new home, a new sporting team or anything else. Write a poem, create a mini-drama or write and perform a dramatic monologue to express your personal **response** to the situation.

Unit 9

Verb tense, quoted (direct) speech, modal verbs

THE 'MOST FAMOUS' FAMOUS LANDMARK

There are many famous built structures in the world.

Many people suggest that the Eiffel Tower in Paris is the most famous of all structures. It is distinctive-looking. It was opened in 1889. It has been famous for well over a hundred years.

Other people believe that the Empire State Building in New York is the most famous building of all. It was finished in 1931 and remained the tallest building in the world until 1972.

I think that the Empire State Building is more famous than the Eiffel Tower. Building the Empire State Building gave people jobs in the Great Depression, and it became an icon of that era. Also, when King Kong climbed it in the movie, it became even more famous.

This **discussion** text includes differing opinions on a topic. It concludes with the writer's opinion. The writer uses a variety of **verbs** and **verb groups** in different **tenses**.

Rule

A **verb group** can include a **modal (auxiliary) verb** to express certainty or obligation.

will go *won't go* *might go* *should go* *must go* *cannot go*

The form of the verb group (including auxiliaries and suffixes) shows tense.

eat *is eating* *eats* *will eat* *did eat* *have eaten* *can't eat* *ate*

1 Read *The 'Most Famous' Famous Landmark*. Underline the **verbs** and **verb groups**.

Write the **saying verb**. ______________________

2 Underline the **verb** or **verb group** in each sentence. Then tick a column to show whether each sentence is **past** or **present tense**. Note that **present tense** is used for activities that are happening now, or that always happen or that are ongoing.

	Past	Present
The Taj Mahal in India is spectacular.		
The Moghul emperor built the Taj Mahal as a tribute to his wife.		
Mt Fuji is the national symbol of Japan.		
Fuji means 'fire' in the language of the indigenous Ainu people.		
The top of the mountain was obscured by clouds.		

3 *The 'Most Famous' Famous Landmark* uses a combination of **past tense verbs** and **present tense verbs**. Find three **past tense verbs/verb groups**.

______________ ______________ ______________

Find three **present tense verbs/verb groups**.

______________ ______________ ______________

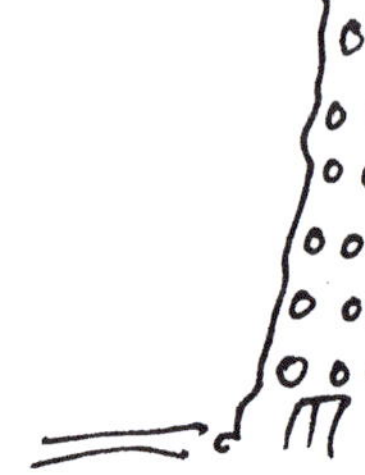

4 Underline the **noun groups** and circle the **verbs** in the sentences below.

The Sydney Opera House is a famous Australian building.

The Sydney Harbour Bridge is a built structure that is world famous.

Australia's Great Barrier Reef and Uluru are two magnificent natural structures.

Grammar Rules! Student Book 6 (ISBN 9780655092544) © Tanya Gibb

5 Write the **verb** forms to show **past tense**.

Base form	Past tense with *–ed* suffix	Past tense with auxiliary
travel	I travelled	I was travelling/did travel
ask	I	I
stop	I	I
visit	I	I
want	I	I

6 Write the **past tense** form of each **irregular verb**.

eat ________________ wear ________________ sing ________________

Quoted or **direct speech** is the actual speech someone said. It is written inside **quotation marks**. Use single quotation marks, but double are also acceptable.
'Hello!' called Mahmoud.

7 Rewrite each sentence with correct punctuation and capital letters.

the statue of liberty is more famous than the empire state building stated logan

____

do you really think so asked aleisha

____

no way interrupted peri the most famous landmark in the world has got to be the sydney harbour bridge ____

____

8 Choose a **modal verb** from the box to support the **future tense** in each sentence.

will	would	could	might

I ______________ love to visit Loch Ness.
I ______________ go to Scotland one day.
Meena and Dougie ______________ come, too.
I ______________ visit my grandma in Edinburgh on the way to Loch Ness.

Interview two classmates or family members. Ask them to nominate their favourite natural or constructed landmark. Write their suggestions and opinions in the form of a written **discussion**. Compare their opinions. Use **quotation marks** if you include quotes.

Unit 10

Reported (indirect) speech, emotive language, synonyms

This online news article includes **reported (indirect) speech** and emotive **vocabulary**.

Top Stories **Just In** **Browse**

SYDNEY SHOWS OFF

By Jessica Cheung Posted 4h ago, updated 3h ago

Hundreds of thousands of people celebrated the new year from vantage points all along the foreshores of Sydney Harbour last night, as fireworks lit the Sydney Harbour Bridge and the Opera House to spectacular effect. Thousands of people started waiting in prime locations, such as Balmain, Kirribilli and Mrs Macquarie's Chair as early as lunchtime yesterday. According to Balmain resident Ravi Barba, the only way to get a good view is to get into position by midday, take all your food and drink supplies for the 13 hours, and stay put. Earlier yesterday, organisers had been concerned about the weather. Strong winds had been predicted but they subsided and allowed the fireworks to proceed. Police said they were kept busy dealing with incidents involving alcohol. However, event organisers said that they were extremely pleased with the evening's celebrations and that the few isolated incidents attended to by police did not impact on the success of the event.

Rule

Reported or **indirect speech** is speech that is not quoted directly. It does not need quotation marks.

1 Read *Sydney Shows Off*. Underline three examples of **reported speech**. Whose speech is reported?

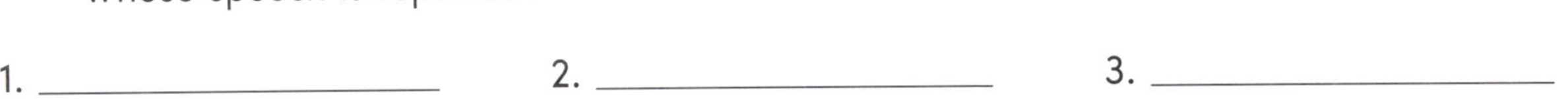

1. ______________ 2. ______________ 3. ______________

2 Rewrite the **quoted speech** as **reported speech**. If you don't know whether the person identifies as 'he/him' or 'she/her', use the pronoun 'they'.

'I love the New Year's Eve fireworks on Sydney Harbour,' said Ravi.

____

'Other cities have fabulous celebrations too,' stated Penny.

____

Gopal said, 'Laser shows are better environmentally than fireworks.'

____

'Melbourne has laser lights coming from the top of city buildings,' bragged Louie.

____

Kala offered, 'My favourite New Year's Eve is watching the sun set on Cable Beach in Western Australia.'

____

Grammar Rules! Student Book 6 (ISBN 9780655092544) © Tanya Gibb

Emotive vocabulary is used to elicit an emotional response from the reader, viewer or listener. It shows the creator's bias about the topic. It is used to sensationalise news reports.

3 *Sydney Shows Off* is a positive headline. Write two alternative headlines for the article that exaggerate the negative police reports. Use **emotive vocabulary**.

______________________ ______________________

Synonyms are words that are similar in meaning.

lean → *skinny* → *thin* → *slender* → *lanky* → *slim*

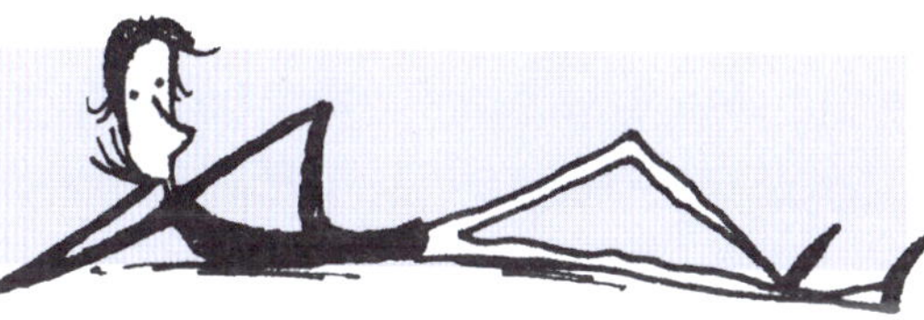

4 Write equally sensational **synonyms** for these words from the article.

spectacular ____________ prime ____________ success ____________

5 Rewrite each news headline to suit the lead paragraph. Use less **emotive vocabulary**.

SCHOOL TEACHES VANDALISM	ELDERLY UNDER SIEGE
______________________	______________________
Eucalypt Valley Public School has announced a new course aimed at teaching students to respect public and private property.	Elderly residents at Pacific Resort for Seniors have been confined to their residences this week due to Council's decision to undertake renovations to their driveways and landscaping.

6 Rewrite the news report below. Replace **quoted speech** with **reported speech**.

Lunar New Year festivities ended last night with the lantern festival. Bystander at the festival, Ruby Nguyen, said, 'Because of my Vietnamese and French heritage, I celebrate Christmas as well as Lunar New Year and have double the fun. I love to visit family and get red envelopes from my aunts and uncles and to wish them luck for the new year.'

____

Write a news report about an event at your school or in your local community. Use **emotive vocabulary** and **reported speech** as well as **quoted speech**. Include a sensational headline to capture readers' attention.

Unit 11

Informal language, contractions, imagery

This postcard uses **informal language** for a familiar audience, as well as **figurative language** and **imagery** to describe the setting.

Greetings from the North-West

Hi Sweetie,

The Buccaneer Archipelago in Western Australia was absolutely beautiful. After that, we had a few days in Broome. Broome's interesting: the Japanese cemetery and the history of pearls here.

The countryside's as red as rust. We've seen lots of boab trees, which we call 'upside-down trees' because it looks like they've been pulled out of the earth and stuck back in upside down with their little roots sticking in the air. We're on our way to Kununurra, now – having a fab time.

Love and bear hugs, from your 'grey nomad' grandparents, Nonna and Poppy.

XOXO

Ms Tatiana Kalishnikova
17 Campbell St
Island Bay 6023
New Zealand

Rule Language varies in **formality** depending on the audience and situation. **Informal language** is used between friends and family and with familiar audiences. It can include **slang** (*barbie* for *barbecue*) and **idiomatic expressions** (*He's feeling under the weather.*).

1 Read *Greetings from the North-West*. Underline any **slang** words or **idiomatic expressions**.

2 What **slang** words or expressions do you use with your friends or family? Write three and their meanings.

____

Tip Formal and informal greetings are used at the start of correspondence and when signing off. What form to use depends on the relationship between the correspondents.

formal	*To whom it may concern*	*Dear Sir/Madam*	*Yours sincerely*
informal	*Hello Darling*	*Dear Mum*	*Love from*

3 Imagine Nonna and Poppy wrote a postcard to ex-work colleagues. It will have more formal language than the postcard to Tatiana. Write what they might say about their trip to this audience.

____

____

____

____

A **contraction** is formed when two words are joined and shortened and a letter or letters are replaced with an **apostrophe**.

is not → isn't *you will → you'll*

An **abbreviation** is a shortened form of a word or words.

continued → cont. *Western Australia → WA*

4 Circle five **contractions** used in *Greetings from the North-West.* Then write each one in its expanded form.

____

5 Write the **simile** in *Greetings from the North-West.*

____

6 Write the expanded form of each **contraction**.

I'm ______________

that's ______________

won't ______________

he'll ______________

7 Write **contractions.** Hint! Remember to use **apostrophes**.

has not ______________

do not ______________

we are ______________

it is ______________

8 Write the **abbreviation** for each term. Hint! You do not need to use **apostrophes**. Check your answers in a dictionary.

New South Wales ______________

Victoria ______________

New Zealand ______________

Avenue ______________

Australian Capital Territory ______________

South Australia ______________

Northern Territory ______________

Tasmania ______________

Road ______________

Highway ______________

Queensland ______________

Street ______________

No punctuation marks are used in addressing mail.
Shortened forms are used for proper nouns:
St Rd Mr Ms
Addresses are written in this order:
name, street, city or suburb, state, postcode, country

9 Write your full name and postal address in the box.

____
____
____
____
____

Imagine you have travelled to an exciting destination. It could be anywhere in the world or a setting from your imagination. Write a postcard or email to a friend or family member. Use **informal language**, **imagery** and **simile** to describe your trip and the scenery.

Unit 12

Revision

1 Draw or describe the situation that is suggested in this sentence.

'This toffee is really sticky, Grandpop. Your teeth might...'

2 Create **noun groups** by completing each table.

Determiner	Number adjective	Descriptive adjective	Noun

Determiner	Number adjective	Noun used to classify	Noun

Possessive adjective	Descriptive adjective	Descriptive adjective	Noun

3 Complete the table.

Adjective	Comparative	Superlative
exciting		
clean		
old		
lazy		
revolting		

4 Underline the **verbs** or **verb groups** in each sentence. Then tick a column to show whether each sentence is **past** or **present tense**.

	Past	Present
Hobart/Nipaluna is a capital city.		
The convicts built Port Arthur.		
The Richmond Bridge was built in 1823.		
It's the oldest bridge in Australia that's still used.		
Penguins have rookeries along the north coast of Tasmania.		
I am researching penguins.		

5 Rewrite each sentence with correct punctuation marks and capital letters.

i'd love to hike around cradle mountain in tasmania said robert

___

it snows there said phoebe

___

tasmanian devils live there offered yanus

___

i don't think you can hike there in the winter suggested ngutapa the snow would be too deep and it might be dangerous

___

___

6 Write a sentence for each **auxiliary verb** in the box.

will
would
could
might

___

___

___

___

7 Rewrite the **quoted speech** as **reported speech**.

'Freycinet National Park is truly stunning,' said Brooke.

___

'I've been camping at Coles Bay,' said Glenn.

___

Hari commented wistfully, 'I'd love to go there.'

___

8 Think of a **colloquial** term for each item.

television ___

car ___

swimwear ___

refrigerator ___

money ___

pyjamas ___

9 Write the expanded form of each **contraction**.

can't ___

they're ___

hasn't ___

she'll ___

10 Write **contractions** with **apostrophes**.

I have ___

do not ___

that is ___

he is ___

Unit 13

Clauses, cohesion, sentence openers

The Deadly Mosquito

Mosquitoes account for more deaths worldwide than any other animal. They can spread diseases, including malaria, yellow fever, Ross River virus, Japanese encephalitis, Zika virus and dengue fever.

Some mosquito-borne diseases can be prevented by vaccines but your best protection against all mosquito-borne diseases is to avoid being bitten by a mosquito.

Follow this advice:

- Stay indoors at dusk.
- Wear long-sleeved shirts, long pants and socks and shoes.
- Use an effective insect repellent.
- Avoid ponds of stagnant water where mosquitoes breed.

Note: Only female mosquitoes bite but they don't really 'bite'. They have a long mouth part (proboscis), which pierces the victim's skin to inject saliva and suck blood.

Tip Sentences can begin with a **noun** or **noun group**, a **pronoun**, a **verb**, an **adverb**, a **prepositional phrase** or a **conjunction**. The way sentences begin can establish **cohesion** in a text (e.g. through noun-pronoun reference) or focus attention on a particular aspect of the message.

1 Underline the first grammatical element in each sentence (also called a **sentence opener**) in *The Deadly Mosquito*.

2 Tick the boxes if any sentences in *The Deadly Mosquito* begin with the following:

☐ a noun or noun group ☐ a pronoun ☐ a verb
☐ an adverb ☐ a prepositional phrase

3 Underline the **sentence openers**.

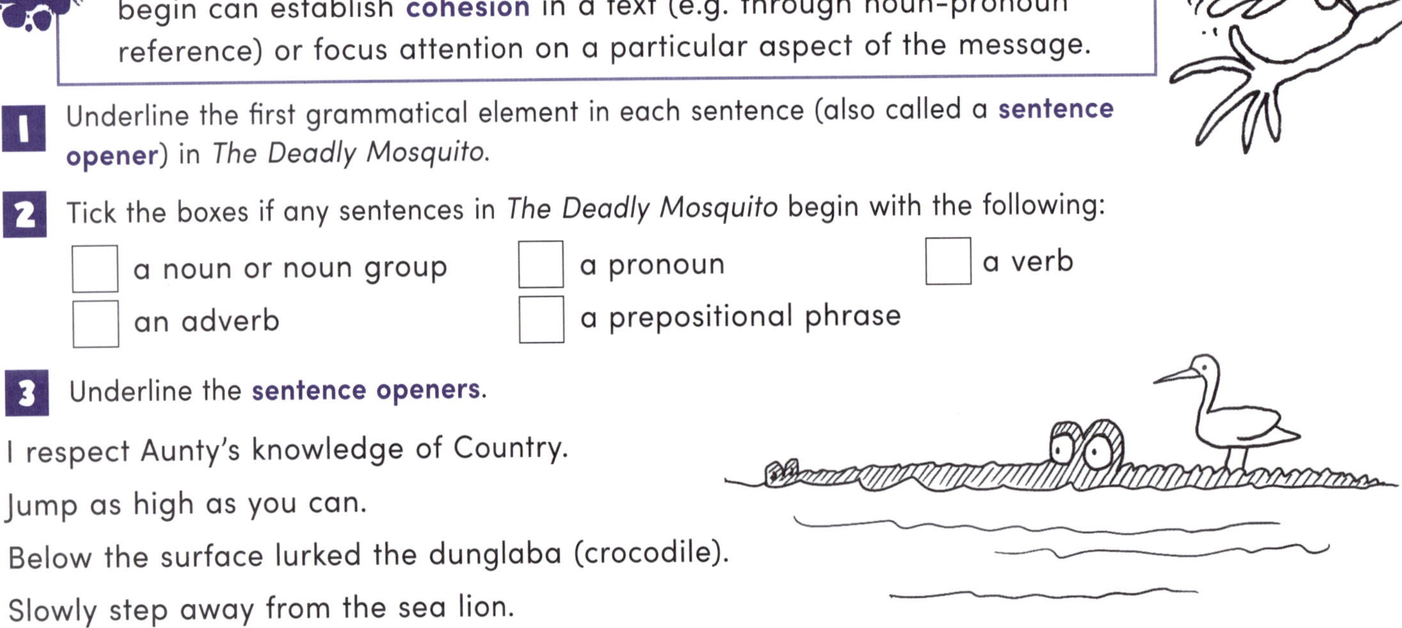

I respect Aunty's knowledge of Country.

Jump as high as you can.

Below the surface lurked the dunglaba (crocodile).

Slowly step away from the sea lion.

Adrienne and Luca went to Gundabooka National Park.

4 Underline the **sentence openers**.

Kakadu National Park is World Heritage listed. Kakadu's Traditional Owners are the Bininj and the Mungguy Peoples. Kakadu has six seasons. They are called Kudjewk, Bangkerreng, Yekke, Wurrkeng, Kurrung and Kunmeleng. Kudjewk is monsoon season.

Grammar Rules! Student Book 6 (ISBN 9780655092544) © Tanya Gibb

Nouns and **pronouns** are used to refer to the same person, place, animal or thing through a text. **Antonyms**, **synonyms** and **word associations** are also used to refer to the same noun.

Crocodiles… They… The prehistoric Deinosuchus… Modern day crocodiles…

5 Draw a / between the **clauses**. Underline the word or word group that begins each clause.

A little penguin colony lives on Phillip Island (Millowl). The little penguins have become Victoria's most popular tourist attraction. The little penguins waddle up the beach to their burrows at sunset. They have been out at sea all day. They bring back fish for their chicks. These small penguins only grow to 33 centimetres.

6 Draw a / between the **clauses**. Underline the word or word group that begins each clause.

Saltwater crocodiles live all along the top of Australia. They can grow quite large and they can be dangerous. They drag their prey under water and do a 'death roll' to drown it. Saltwater crocodiles have been known to attack people. Tourists are advised to be wary of them, especially when camping and fishing.

7 This **procedure** is not written clearly. Rewrite it so that **doing verbs** begin each **clause**. Write the steps in a logical sequence. Use dot points.

When driving a car, there are some safety rules for a safe journey. You need to wear a seatbelt. You need to keep your eyes on the road. You must always stay at a safe distance from the vehicle in front. You can't talk on a mobile phone. Don't eat a hamburger while you drive. If you have to turn a corner, you need to indicate. Don't travel faster than the speed limit. You can't just stop in the middle of the road. When you need to stop, you have to pull over to the side of the road first.

Write a **procedure** for something that you know how to do, such as repairing a bike tyre, organising a school assembly or playing a game. Write the procedure as a series of steps in logical order. Use **verbs** or **adverbs** to begin each clause.

Unit 14

Pronouns, clauses, connectives

Curse of the Pharaohs

Egypt used to be my favourite place in the world until the day my life was changed forever – the day when the curse struck! My parents are journalists and my brother and I often travel with them. I loved it when they went to Egypt. It was so mysterious. Jack and I used to fool around and pretend we were being chased by possessed mummies or trapped in undiscovered tombs, until one day, we didn't have to pretend.

It all began when my parents had to interview an archaeologist at the Great Pyramid of Giza. Jack and I wandered away, underground, through the maze of tunnels under the pyramid, and it wasn't long before we became lost. We found ourselves in a room in the pyramid we'd never seen before. Hieroglyphics decorated the walls, and the eyes of the god, Horus, looked down on us from the granite ceiling. We stood transfixed by the eyes as the air became chilly and a stone wall slammed across our exit. We were trapped!

This text is the beginning of a **narrative**. It is written in the first person from the perspective of one of the characters. It establishes the **setting** for the story.

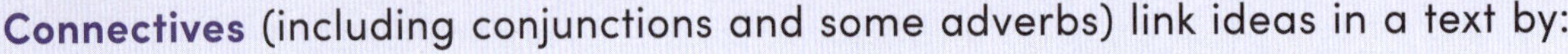

Rule

Connectives (including conjunctions and some adverbs) link ideas in a text by:

- adding information — *in addition*, *as well as*
- providing a reason or cause — *because*, *therefore*, *so*
- expressing a condition — *even though*, *if*, *unless*
- sequencing in time or logically. — *firstly*, *finally*, *while*

A **comma** is used to separate a dependent clause from a main clause if the dependent clause comes first in the sentence.

1 Read *Curse of the Pharaohs*. Circle the **connectives** *(until, when, and, when, and, or, until, when, and, before, and, as, and).*

2 Rewrite each pair of sentences as a single sentence with a **connective**. Hint! The **connective** might go at the beginning of either **clause**.

because as well as but

We were frightened of mummies. We were frightened of curses.

____

I was worried. I knew my parents would look for us.

____

A stone wall moved by itself to block our exit. We became trapped.

____

Grammar Rules! Student Book 6 (ISBN 9780655092544) © Tanya Gibb

3 Write whether the underlined **connective** in each sentence functions to add information, give a condition, show cause or show a time sequence.

<u>As well as</u> the pyramids, the Sphinx has also survived in the dry climate. ______________________

The air in the desert is extremely dry. <u>Therefore</u> pyramids have survived for centuries.

____

Pyramids may have survived the weather <u>but</u> many did not survive vandals. ______________________

The children were trapped. <u>Meanwhile</u>, in another part of the pyramid, their parents were interviewing Dr Bakhari. ______________________

Rule

Who, whom, whose, which and *that* are **relative pronouns**. They are used to refer to nouns already mentioned in a text. They can be used to form **complex sentences**.

We stayed with cousins. They live in Albury. → We stayed with cousins who live in Albury.

4 Add a relative **pronoun**.

We found ourselves in a room ______________ we'd never seen before.

5 Rewrite each pair of sentences as a single sentence using a **relative pronoun** from the box.

who which whose that

My uncle is an archaeologist. He lives in Lebanon.

____

The journalist's job was to interview the archaeologist. The journalist was on holiday.

____

The museum housed artefacts from the pyramids. The museum was closed.

____

The souvenir stall was closed. It sold pottery pyramids.

____

6 Rewrite each pair of sentences as a single sentence. Use a **connective** or a **relative pronoun** to join the **clauses**.

My parents interviewed an archaeologist. The archaeologist specialised in hieroglyphics.

____

I loved hearing about Egypt. It is so mysterious.

____

Try it yourself!

Write an ending for the **narrative** *Curse of the Pharaohs*. Use a variety of sentence types. Short, **simple sentences** can increase the pace of the action and suspense. **Complex sentences** can help create detailed and interesting **setting** and **character** descriptions.

Unit 15 Complex sentences, clauses, relating verbs

This text provides a list of recommendations. It includes **dependent clauses** that add extra information to **main (independent) clauses**.

Travel Tips

The Australian government Smart Traveller website advises Australian travellers on ways to reduce risk and avoid problems when travelling overseas.

- Check the website to avoid dangerous destinations.
- Obey local laws.
- Be culturally sensitive and aware of local norms and customs, including wearing appropriate clothing.
- Wear a hat, sunscreen and comfortable shoes.
- Drink bottled water when tap water is not considered safe to drink.
- Avoid ice in drinks unless it is made from bottled water.
- Eat cooked vegetables and avoid salads.
- Eat fruit that you can peel, such as bananas and pineapples.

Rule

Dependent clauses depend on a **main (independent) clause** for meaning. A dependent clause can function as an adjective or an adverb.

Eat the mango that is ripe. The dependent (adjectival) clause describes the mango.

You should cross where there's a zebra crossing. The dependent (adverbial) clause tells place (where).

1 Read *Travel Tips*. Underline a **complex sentence** that includes a dependent clause. What information does the dependent clause add?

____

Tip Remember the rule on page 35.

2 Finish the **clause** at the end of each sentence.

Ask for advice from a person who ______________________________

Wear a hat that ______________________________

Wear sunscreen that ______________________________

I'll be wearing my black hiking boots, which ______________________________

Avoid drinks that ______________________________

Eat fruit that ______________________________

Enjoy cultural experiences that ______________________________

Travel to places where ______________________________

Grammar Rules! Student Book 6 (ISBN 9780655092544) © Tanya Gibb

Relating (being) verbs show relationships. You cannot see any action taking place.
is belongs represents equals was had are have

3 Write the **relating verb** on the line.

Smart Traveller ____________ a government website.

4 Use a **relating verb** from the box to complete each sentence.

become belongs equal are had

We ______________ a great holiday.
Tadpoles ______________ frogs.
My dog and your dog ______________ trouble.
Bears ______________ mammals.
The seat ______________ here.

5 Write a sentence for each **relating verb** in the box.

is has becomes represents belongs

____
____
____
____
____

6 Find and write a **connective** in *Travel Tips* that adds a condition to a **main clause**. ______________

7 Add a **clause** to finish each sentence about safe travel.

Because you forgot to wear sunscreen, ______________________
You'll get a tummy ache ______________________
You should wear comfortable walking shoes ______________________
You can upset people ______________________

8 Connect the clauses to create one **complex sentence**. Write the new sentence.

The park has significant cultural and ecological value. These need to be protected. The impacts of wildfires, weeds, feral animals and erosion need to be managed.

____
____

Create a leaflet or brochure of advice for travellers within Australia. Write a list of recommendations about cultural sensitivity. For example: *Do not enter or photograph restricted areas, sacred sites or burial grounds.* Construct **complex sentences** to extend or explain the recommendations.

Unit 16 Emotive vocabulary, modal verbs and adverbs

This **persuasive text** is a travel advertisement. It uses **emotive vocabulary** and **commands** to persuade readers to take action.

COME TO CHINA!

This outstanding, value-for-money, 12-day tour is available ***today*** *to the first 100 callers only.*

Travel in a small exclusive group to Beijing, Guilin, Shanghai and Xi'an.

DISCOVER amazing historical sites:
the Great Wall of China, the Forbidden City, the Li River, the Terracotta Warriors.

Tour includes **premium** transport, food and accommodation – everything you need.

Once-in-a-lifetime opportunity – Don't miss out!
GUARRANTEE your place on the tour today.
Book NOW. It's easy.

China Tours on 1 700 791 791

Tip Speakers and writers sometimes use **emotive vocabulary** to make their audience feel emotions such as guilt, anger or greed in order to persuade them to do something.
Buy now or you'll miss out. *Every child needs one.* *Plastic kills innocent animals.*

1 Read *Come to China!* Highlight the **emotive** words and phrases.

2 Write the emotive words in *Come to China!* that are **descriptive adjectives**.

___

How are these **descriptive adjectives** meant to make the reader feel?

___

3 Why might the advertisement say *Come to China!* rather than *Go to China!*?

___

4 Use a thesaurus to find more **emotive synonyms** to replace the underlined words. Rewrite each line.

Tip Remember the rule on page 27.

Termites <u>move in</u> and <u>damage</u> local homes.

___

The elderly <u>experience</u> neglect.

___

Climate <u>problems</u> cause <u>some</u> bushfires in Australia.

___

Grammar Rules! Student Book 6 (ISBN 9780655092544) © Tanya Gibb

Modal verbs (e.g. *will, won't, might, might not, should, can't*) and **modal adverbs** (e.g. *definitely, possibly, probably*) help to express how certain, likely or possible a happening is.

I will go. *I'll probably go.* *I really should go.*

I might not go. *I definitely won't go.*

5 The advertisement *Come to China!* is **persuasive** because it uses words that express certainty. Rewrite each line below using less persuasive terms.

Very certain	Less certain
Now is the best time.	______________
You will travel in a small group.	______________
You will see amazing sites.	______________
This tour always includes all transport.	______________
This is a once-in-a-lifetime opportunity.	______________
It should not be missed.	______________
Book your tour today.	______________

What effect would less certain language have on a reader of the advertisement?

____

____

6 Rewrite each sentence using more certain language.

I could come to your house. ______________

I might go to the library after school. ______________

I don't think it's going to rain today. ______________

It may be too late to buy a ticket. ______________

We'll probably have a great trip. ______________

They probably won't come to China with us. ______________

I don't understand your reasoning. ______________

7 Why might the advertisement make the promise *available* *today* *to the first 100 callers only?*

____

Record *Come to China!* as a radio advertisement. Use your voice to persuade. Try to sound very convincing and certain. Add music and sound effects if you can. Or, write a **persuasive** text in the form of a travel advertisement for somewhere you have been or would like to go.

Unit 17

Complex sentences, clauses, prepositional phrases, imagery

This response text includes **complex sentences** and **adjectives** to describe a place.

Uluru

I recently visited Uluru on Anangu Country with my family. It is the most incredible place that I have ever seen. Uluru stands 340 metres tall, and it is 9.4 kilometres around its base. The rock probably extends five or six kilometres under the ground, so only a small percentage of the rock is above the surface, like an iceberg.

It is really amazing when Uluru changes colour during the different stages of the day, such as sunset and sunrise. The play of light on the rock is a fascinating sight. The rock appears to change colour from red to bright orange to a dark, deep burnt orange, to shades of purple and mauve. The vast, open, flat land around Uluru is also very beautiful. It is filled with small native shrubs and flowers that miraculously survive in the dry red earth. Uluru–Kata Tjuta National Park is World Heritage listed. I can understand why.

1 Write five **adjectives** that allow you to know the writer's opinion of Uluru.

____

2 Read *Uluru*. Underline the **verbs** and **verb groups**.

3 Circle the **conjunctions** *and* and *so* in the first paragraph of *Uluru*. Circle the correct words in brackets: Each conjunction links two (**dependent/independent**) clauses in a (**compound/complex**) sentence.

4 Write the **simile** used in *Uluru*. ______________________________

Why is this imagery effective? ______________________________

5 How would you feel about the events described below if you were an Anangu person? Write a response.

Uluru means 'great pebble' in the language of its Traditional Owners, the Anangu people. The rock was created by ancestral spirits in the Dreamtime. Uluru has been a very important sacred place for tens of thousands of years to the Anangu people. In 1873, the government took control of Uluru away from the traditional owners and renamed it Ayers Rock after Sir Henry Ayers, who was chief secretary of South Australia at the time. Ownership of the site was not returned to the Anangu people until 1985, and the rock's name was officially changed back to Uluru in 1995.

____

____

____

Grammar Rules! Student Book 6 (ISBN 9780655092544) © Tanya Gibb

Grammar Rules!

_______________________ 's Writing Log

1 Plan

What is the purpose of the text?
Who is the audience?
What text structure and features will you use?
What mode or medium will enhance the presentation?
Gather ideas or research the topic, including using online and digital sources.

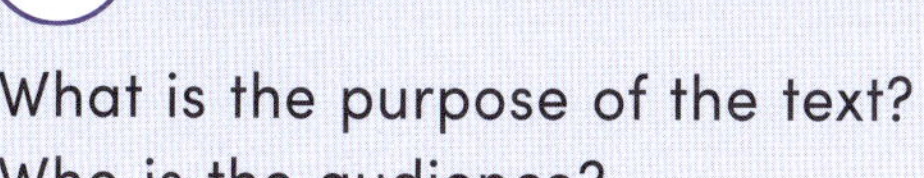

2 Draft

Gather and organise your ideas.
Use a graphic organiser or digital tools.
Compose your text.

3 Edit/Revise

Are you using the best text structure and language features for your intended purpose and audience?

Are your ideas well-sequenced with appropriate connectives?

Have you used sentence openers and pronouns effectively for cohesion?

Have you used topic-specific and vivid vocabulary?

Will your text engage your audience?

Can you explain your editing choices if required?

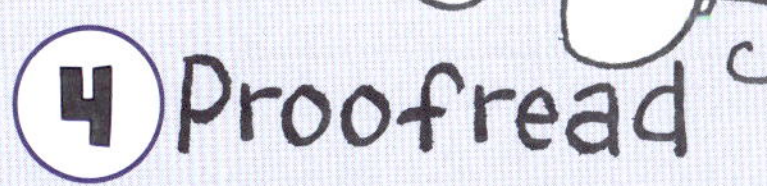

4 Proofread

Check grammar and punctuation.
Check homophones are correct.
Use online dictionaries to check spelling.

5 Publish

Consider layout, other visual features and auditory aspects.
Use digital tools.
Reflect on your work.

Create symbols for a rating scale. Then each time you finish a piece of writing, record it in the log.

My rating scale

Symbol	Meaning
☐	______ ______
☐	______ ______
☐	______ ______
☐	______ ______
☐	______ ______

Do you need some ideas for other text forms to try? Look at the back page!

Date	Write the title of your text.	Text purpose and structure	Audience
Write the date.	Write the title of your piece.	e.g. recount/ email	Who were you writing for or to

Grammar Rules! Student Book 6 (ISBN 9780655092544) © Tanya Gibb

Language features	My rating	Where to next?
st the main grammar and other language atures that you used.	Record your rating.	What language features could you try next? How could you improve your text? Does your teacher have any comments?

I've tried these types of texts and text forms . . .

Narrative

- [ ] Story
- [ ] Play script
- [ ] Comic
- [ ] Ballad
- [ ] Retelling a story
- [ ] Poem
- [ ] Song
- [ ] Other ____________________

Recount

- [ ] Letter/email
- [ ] Biography
- [ ] Autobiography
- [ ] News article
- [ ] Imaginative recount
- [ ] Other ____________________

Description

- [ ] Poem
- [ ] Story
- [ ] Play script
- [ ] Biography
- [ ] Advertisement
- [ ] Narrative/story
- [ ] Other ____________________

Informative

- [ ] Information report
- [ ] Website/brochure/leaflet/poster
- [ ] Magazine article
- [ ] Documentary
- [ ] Biography
- [ ] Other ____________________

Procedure

- [ ] Recipe
- [ ] Instructions
- [ ] Rules
- [ ] Directions

Explanation

- [ ] Magazine article
- [ ] Cycle diagram/flow chart
- [ ] Digital chart

Persuasion

- [ ] Debate
- [ ] Argument/speech
- [ ] Letter to editor
- [ ] Editorial
- [ ] TV advertisement
- [ ] Magazine advertisement
- [ ] Radio advertisement
- [ ] Leaflet
- [ ] Music video
- [ ] Blog
- [ ] Poem/song lyrics
- [ ] Other ____________________

Discussion

- [ ] Conversation
- [ ] TV interview
- [ ] Talkback radio
- [ ] Dialogue in a story
- [ ] Panel discussion
- [ ] Formal interview
- [ ] Other ____________________

Response/Reflection

- [ ] Review (film, book, concert, excursion)
- [ ] Diary or journal
- [ ] Poem
- [ ] Other ____________________

Grammar Rules! Student Book 6 (ISBN 9780655092544) © Tanya Gibb

6 Rewrite each set of simple sentences as one sentence.

The Anangu people welcome tourists. Tourists need to respect Anangu culture. Tourists need to recognise Uluru as a site of spiritual significance to the Anangu people.

Uluru changes colour in different weather and at different times of day. It is always a spectacular sight in any colour.

---

7 Use **relative pronouns** (e.g. *who, which, that*) or **conjunctions** to join these three sentences into a single sentence.

People are advised not to bring plants or seeds into the national park. People are not allowed to camp in the national park. People should take their rubbish with them when they leave the national park.

---

8 Re-read question 7. Evaluate the effect of using three shorter sentences compared with one **compound** or **complex sentence**. Which do you prefer? Why?

Remember the rule on page 14.

9 Circle the **prepositional phrase** in each sentence.

It is a sight for sore eyes.

The man beside the road has lost his dog.

The climber in red thongs is having difficulty.

The play of light on the rock is a fascinating sight.

The vast, open, flat land around Uluru is also very beautiful.

The native plants with the small yellow flowers are my favourites.

Create a **response** about something that interests you. It could be a song, a person or a place. Use **compound** and **complex sentences**. Build up your noun groups using **adjectival phrases**. Publish your text online using photos or film clips.

Unit 18

Revision

1 Add an interesting word or word group to each sentence.

__________ got into my television.

__________ to Perth for your next holiday.

The goat escaped __________.

__________ back away from the snarling bear.

__________ are cousins but they look like sisters.

2 Circle the **nouns** and **pronouns** used to refer to the reef.

The Ningaloo Reef is off the coast of Western Australia. Ningaloo Reef is home to over 520 species of fish. It is famous for its whale shark. The whale sharks migrate to Ningaloo Reef at certain times of the year. The reef is also home to green, loggerhead, hawk's bill and flatback turtles.

3 Circle the words that refer to Perth. Underline the words that refer to quokkas.

Perth is the capital city of Western Australia. It is situated on the Swan River, approximately 20 kilometres inland from the Indian Ocean. A short ferry ride away from Perth is Rottnest Island, where you can see quokkas. These are small marsupials. They can become quite tame.

4 Write an advertisement to encourage students your age to enrol at your school. Use **emotive language**. Describe the image that would best support your advertisement.

____

____

____

____

5 Complete each **dependent clause** to describe the underlined noun.

When out in the sun, wear a hat that __________

While hiking in the desert, wear sensible shoes that __________

Eat a healthy breakfast that __________

To do your best work, sit with a reliable classmate who __________

6 Rewrite each statement to express less certainty.

Very certain	Less certain
You must visit now.	__________
You will have a great time.	__________
You won't be late.	__________
It must be finished.	__________
I cannot allow it.	__________

Grammar Rules! Student Book 6 (ISBN 9780655092544) © Tanya Gibb

7 Use a **relating verb** from the box to complete each sentence.

become belong equal are had

Cygnets ____________ swans.

We ____________ a terrific time in Perth.

Whale sharks ____________ not dangerous.

The muddy footprints ____________ to me.

My sister and your sister ____________ trouble.

8 Add an **independent clause** to complete each **compound sentence**.

I like train travel but ______________________________

You can catch a bus or ______________________________

Archie felt ill so ______________________________

I'll get an ice cream and ______________________________

9 Write a less **emotive** synonym for each word. Use a dictionary or thesaurus.

horrendous ____________________ vindictive ____________________

tragedy ____________________ incarcerated ____________________

10 Create **complex sentences**. Use **pronouns** and **conjunctions** to join each group of **simple sentences**.

I watched the sun set on Uluru. The colour changes were dramatic. I was surprised. All the tourists were quiet and respectful of the site.

____

____

Feral animals prey on small native species of mammals in the national park. The feral animals are cats and foxes. A number of native species have become extinct.

____

____

11 Underline the **prepositional phrase** in each sentence.

The countryside around Uluru is red and flat.

The water at Ningaloo Reef is turquoise.

The tourist without a hat is very sunburnt.

The chocolate wrappers under the table are not mine.

12 Add an **prepositional phrase** after each main **noun**.

The humpback ____________________ is travelling with its baby.

The performer ____________________ is my favourite.

Bill prefers the tie ____________________.

Sharne and Costas like the goldfish ____________________.

Unit 19

Subjective/objective language, possessive apostrophes

In this **persuasive** text, the writer supports an opinion with facts and reasoning.

Where Would You Go?

The place in the world that I would most like to visit is Antarctica.

The main reason I choose it as my favourite destination is that I would love to see the animals in their natural habitat. There are seven different penguin species living in Antarctica – rockhopper, king, macaroni, emperor, gentoo, chinstrap and Adélie, plus other large sea birds, such as albatrosses. There are five species of seals – the crabeater, Weddell, leopard, Ross and southern elephant seals. There are whales – the southern right, the humpback, and the blue, fin and sei whales. All these animals fascinate me.

Secondly, I would love to see the colours and shapes of the ice: the natural ice sculptures, the glaciers and icebergs. The ice looks spectacular in photos and in documentaries.

These are the reasons that I would love to visit Antarctica more than any other place in the world. I think you would love it too.

1 Read *Where Would You Go?* Summarise the two main reasons given by the writer for choosing Antarctica as their favourite destination. List the facts given to support each main reason.

Reason	Supporting facts

Objective language is factual and not emotive or biased. **Subjective language** shows personal opinions, judgements and bias. Sometimes what appears to be a fact is really an opinion.

2 Tick a column to show whether each statement is **objective** or **subjective**.

	Objective	Subjective
Antarctica is under threat of human exploitation.		
Antarctica and Australia were once attached.		
Douglas Mawson established a base in Antarctica in 1912.		
Antarctic wildlife needs conservation programs.		

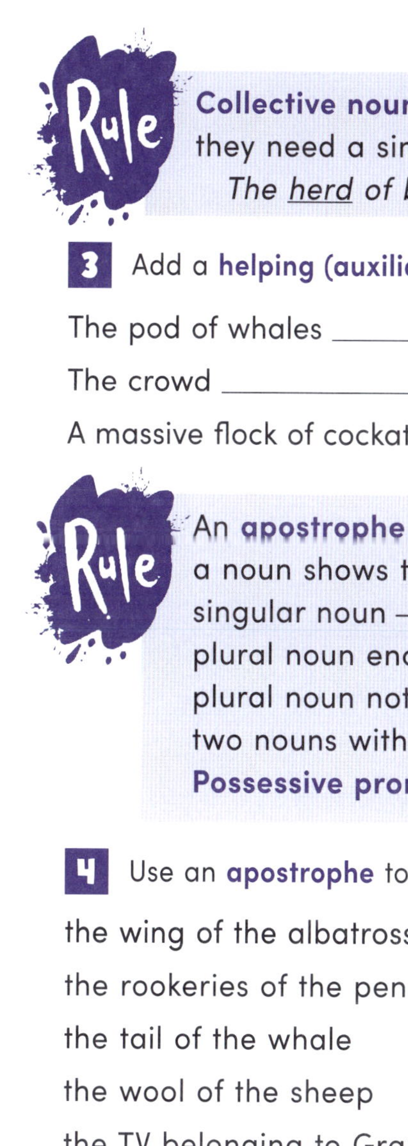

Collective nouns are names for groups of things. Collective nouns are **singular**, so they need a singular verb.

The herd of brumbies is heading for the waterhole. *The bouquet has wilted.*

3 Add a **helping (auxiliary) verb** to each line to complete the **verb group**.

The pod of whales ______________ migrating north.

The crowd ______________ surging towards the exits as the game ended.

A massive flock of cockatoos ______________ just flown overhead.

An **apostrophe** can show possession. An apostrophe with a noun shows that something belongs to that noun.

singular noun → add *'s* *rhinoceros's*

plural noun ending in *s* → add *'* *babies'*

plural noun not ending in *s* → add *'s* *children's*

two nouns with equal ownership → add *'s* to the second noun *Betty and Jim's house*

Possessive pronouns do not have apostrophes. *hers his theirs its*

4 Use an **apostrophe** to write the possessive form of the each noun.

the wing of the albatross	the ______________ wing
the rookeries of the penguins	______________
the tail of the whale	______________
the wool of the sheep	______________
the TV belonging to Granny and Pa	______________

Tip

Cohesion is created by using **word associations** that link content across a text.

minke whale → baleen whale → whale → sea mammal → mammal → vertebrate → animal

5 Write a set of **nouns** or **noun groups** to label a place of your choice. Use the example in the Tip as a reference.

6 Write a set of **nouns** or **noun groups** for the following.

emperor penguin → ______________________________

droplet of water → ______________________________

Create a text that presents your opinion about something you would like to do. Include your reasons. Support your reasons with facts and opinions. Use **objective** and **subjective language**. Try to convince others to agree with your opinion. Add images and create a short slide show to present to the class.

This text is a **parody** of an advertisement. It makes fun of real estate advertising by using words and phrases that are commonly found in these types of texts.

Land Sale!

Own a piece of the largest desert in Australia: the Great Victoria Desert, which spans South Australia and Western Australia.

Guaranteed never to flood.

Just a helicopter flight to shops, schools and restaurants.

Experience warm days and cool desert nights.

Find solitude, peace and tranquillity.

POTENTIAL PLUS! REDEVELOP AS A MINE.

This is a once-in-a-lifetime opportunity to invest in a pristine wilderness.

Get in now or miss out forever!

Contact Burke and Wills Realty for your last chance to buy

– a perfect portion of paradise.

Tip A **parody** is when a familiar text is imitated but changed in a way to make fun of it. To fully understand a parody, the reader needs to be familiar with the type of text that is being imitated. Exaggeration can also add to the humour in a parody.

1 Read *Land Sale!* It is a **parody** of a real estate advertisement. Underline words and phrases that might typically be found in a real estate advertisement.

2 What words and phrases in the ad let the reader know that *Land Sale!* is not serious?

3 Do some research. Who were Burke and Wills? Why would the author of *Land Sale!* use Burke and Wills in the parody?

4 Do some research about the Great Victoria Desert. Why might the author of *Land Sale!* choose the Great Victoria Desert to advertise in this parody?

Tip **Alliteration** is when the beginnings of words sound the same. Alliteration can sound pleasing or contribute to mood or rhythm in a text.

stealthy shadows slunk *dust mites danced in the dappled light*

5 Write the examples of **alliteration** used in *Land Sale!*.

Grammar Rules! Student Book 6 (ISBN 9780655092544) © Tanya Gibb

Fractured tales are examples of parody. In a fractured tale, the traditional tale is revised in any number of ways, including changing the gender or point of view of characters or altering the plot or the setting. Knowledge of the traditional tale helps readers to appreciate the humour in the parody.

6 Plan a **parody** of the fairytale *Cinderella*. You might like to work with a partner. How could you change the story to make it funny or more applicable to modern times? Write your ideas in the boxes. A parody could be based on changing one area or more than one.

Cinderella	Traditional tale		Parody	
PLOT SUMMARY	A young woman is bullied by family. She dreams of going to a fancy ball. A fairy godmother helps her. She meets a prince and they fall in love.			
CHARACTERS	Kind Cinderella	Evil family members		
POINT OF VIEW	The main character's (the reader/viewer feels sorry for her)			
SETTING	Place: A fantasy kingdom			
	Time: A long time ago			
LANGUAGE	Once upon a time			
RESOLUTION	Cinderella marries a prince and they live happily every after.			

Work with classmates to create your own **parody** of a traditional tale (fairytale, folk tale or nursery rhyme). Read some fractured fairytales for ideas. Present your parody as a digital text or podcast to an audience. Use language typically found in traditional tales, along with descriptive words and phrases of your own.

Unit 21

Cohesion, word associations, articles

A FUTURE

Yousif's grandparents
Greece
migrants 1949
engineered a miracle
in the Snowy Mountains.

Dijana's parents
Bosnia
refugees 1999
created a home
far from 'home'.

Tan Le's family
Vietnam
refugees 1977
came by boat
for a new life.

Mohamed
Iraq
asylum seeker 2007
made friends
in Australia.

Tip

Definite article: *the* used for a particular thing or things.
Look at the trees. Pass the apple.
Indefinite article: *a, an* used for things in general.
Pass me an apple. Buy a watermelon.

1 Read *A Future*. The poet used *A* in the title rather than *The*. What does *A Future* imply?

____

____

2 What is the main idea in the poem?

____

3 Write a **definite** or **indefinite article** to complete each sentence.

We are planning __________ trip to Katherine Gorge/Nitmiluk.
__________ trip to Winton has been cancelled.
I need __________ answer by Friday.
Do you know __________ answer to the quiz?
Buy __________ juice with the gold sticker.
May I have __________ turn?

Grammar Rules! Student Book 6 (ISBN 9780655092544) © Tanya Gibb

Noun groups, word associations, synonyms and antonyms help make a text **cohesive**.

Uluru → spectacular site → ancient rock → monolith

Antonyms are words with opposite meanings.

4 Write the words and word groups that follow the pattern and make *A Future* **cohesive**.

family groups: ______

countries: ______

labels for people arriving in Australia: ______

years: ______

verbs: ______

final phrases: ______

5 Write a new five-line stanza for *A Future* based on your own family. Follow the pattern in *A Future*.

______

______

______

______

______

6 Circle the **noun groups** for locations in the text below. These show part-whole word associations.

My name is Gabriella. I have a yellow bedroom inside a red brick house. My suburb is Five Dock in the city of Sydney. My state is New South Wales in the country of Australia. I live on the planet called Earth in a universe that goes on forever.

7 Write a third stanza for the poem below. Follow the pattern.

Night descended softly.	Morning pounced with a clang.	______
Sneaking up,	Crashing down,	______
stealthily enveloping	harshly illuminating	______
my senses.	my thoughts.	______

8 Rewrite the sentences with correct punctuation.

ayul said when i came to australia from south sudan I went to school made friends and learned english

______

______

Write a poem using **antonyms** and/or **synonyms** and other word associations to create a pattern. Include words and phrases that will help readers make mental pictures. Your poem can be a description or a response to a news item, a weather event or any topic of your choice.

Mummification

The ancient Egyptians developed the process of mummification to preserve bodies for life after death.

First, the brain was removed by pushing a hook up the nose and dragging it out. Then the empty skull was rinsed with preservatives. Next, the internal organs were removed and sealed away in special storage jars called Canopic jars. After that, the empty shell of the body was dried out for 40 days using salt-like preservatives. When dried out sufficiently, the body was then stuffed with salt and sweet-smelling oiled rags to give it a human shape again. Artificial eyes were then stuck on and the body was coated with resin. Finally, it was wrapped in hundreds of metres of linen bandage strips soaked with more resin. Magic charms, decorations and amulets were then attached to the mummy before it was placed inside a decorated wooden coffin.

1 Read *Mummification*. Underline the ten **connectives** that show a time sequence.

2 Explanations often include diagrams or flow charts. Draw a ten-cell flow diagram to show each step in the process of mummification. Add a label to each cell.

Remember the rule on page 34.

______ ______	______ ______	______ ______	______ ______	______ ______
______ ______	______ ______	______ ______	______ ______	______ ______

Grammar Rules! Student Book 6 (ISBN 9780655092544) © Tanya Gibb

3 Rewrite each sentence with correct punctuation. Hint! Look out for **possessive nouns** that need apostrophes.

the ancient egyptians believed that the dead persons body needed to be preserved for the journey into the afterlife announced xanthe

the chinchorro peoples, the incas and other ancient south american civilisations also practised mummification replied pablo

australias early peoples used mummification in rituals too on mainland australia and in the torres strait said matt

listen to this maddy the chincorro people mummified their dead to preserve them so they could visit them and bring them food and other gifts said mo

4 Some horror stories involve Egyptian mummies, curses and adventures. Create a comic strip story involving a mummy. Plan your narrative on spare paper, then choose six key moments to draw here. Add time labels or speech bubbles.

Write an **explanation** for a topic of your choice. For example: How a volcano erupts. You might like to work with a partner. Use **connectives** to link information through cause and effect. Create a flow diagram for the sequence of information.

Unit 23

Sentences, idiom, first- and third-person pronouns, flashback

This text is the beginning of a **third-person narrative**. It introduces the main **character** and the **setting** for the events to follow.

The Accidental Traveller

'Violet, I need you to get my good shoes from the garage!' yelled Violet's mother from across the hallway.

Violet slumped down the stairs, grumbling to herself and entered the garage. She quickly spotted the silver shoes on the ground and stooped to get them. As she stood up, she bumped a shelf and something small, but heavy, fell from the shelf onto her back and then onto the floor. It was a small, cube-shaped object with one large button that had been bumped to 'on'.

Violet's vision started to blur and she felt a piercing stab behind her eyes. She pressed her hands to her eyes and the pain eventually subsided, but when she opened her eyes, she was standing in front of a building she recognised from a postcard her grandparents had once sent her.

Someone shouted, 'Move!' and Violet jumped aside, narrowly avoiding being hit by a horse-drawn carriage. It dawned on her that she was no longer in the garage at home.

1 Underline the **verbs** that tell you that Violet was reluctant to run the errand to the garage. Why might she be reluctant? ____

____

2 Circle the **personal pronouns** in *The Accidental Traveller*. Who or what do the following third-person pronouns refer to in *The Accidental Traveller*?

I __________________ She __________________ them __________________

her __________________ It __________________ It __________________

3 What does the **idiom** *it dawned on her* mean?

____

4 What does the title *The Accidental Traveller* imply?

____

5 Underline a **compound sentence** in *The Accidental Traveller*. Highlight the **conjunction** in the sentence.

6 Summarise the events in the plot so far.

____

____

Narratives can be written in the **first person** from the perspective of one of the characters. The character uses the pronoun 'I' to tell readers how they think and feel about events and about other characters. Narratives can also be written in the **third person**, so the author tells what any or all of the characters think and feel, using the pronouns 'he', 'she', 'it' and 'they'.

7 Rewrite paragraph 3 from *The Accidental Traveller* in the **first person** with Violet as narrator. Tell Violet's thoughts and feelings.

8 What kind of events can you predict might occur in the rest of the narrative?

Tip

Flashback is a literary device that authors use to tell readers about something that happened before the story commenced or earlier in the story. A flashback can explain a character's reaction to something in the story.

9 Write a **flashback** for *The Accidental Traveller* in which Violet remembers how the *small cube-shaped object with one large button* came to be in the garage.

10 Rewrite the text below in the **third person**.

Jess: 'I'm excited about visiting family in Wagga Wagga for the school holidays. It's Wiradjuri Country, and when I visit, my Aunty teaches me about Country.'

11 Find and write six **prepositional phrases** used in *The Accidental Traveller* that tell place.

Write a **third-person narrative**. Describe the **characters** and the **setting**. Make sure the **plot** is interesting for readers. You might like to write a time travel story of your own. How does your main character travel and where?

Unit 24 Revision

1 Write a **subjective** statement to suit each factual or **objective** statement.

Copenhagen is the capital city of Denmark.

____

A famous landmark in Copenhagen is the small bronze statue of the Little Mermaid.

____

In winter, the average temperature in Copenhagen is 0°C.

____

2 Add a **helping (auxiliary) verb** to each line.

The swarm __________ heading back to the hive.

The bees __________ been feasting in the sunflower fields.

A bee __________ sitting on a lavender flower.

My team __________ coming first in the competition.

3 Write words and phrases as substitutes for 'echidna' in an imaginative text.

____

____

____

____

4 Rewrite each line using an **apostrophe** to show possession.

the horns of the rhinoceros _______________

the nest of the magpies _______________

the wheelchair belonging to Ethan _______________

the bags of the children _______________

the car belonging to Mum and Dad _______________

5 Rewrite the paragraph below for a **third-person** narrative.

My colleague Kiko called out to me as I peered into the sarcophagus. 'Yuriy, don't disturb anything.' I told her I wouldn't. She was being cautious. We'd heard rumours about a mummy.

____

____

____

6 Circle the **verb groups** and underline the **prepositional phrases**.

The tourists viewed Nitmiluk Gorge from the water.

Jawoyn rangers care for this Country.

The whole wattle seed cake was gorged by the family.

Rock art surveys are conducted by Nitmiluk National Park rangers.

Grammar Rules! Student Book 6 (ISBN 9780655092544) © Tanya Gibb

7 Write two **synonyms** for each of the following words to create word banks. Use a thesaurus.

ecstatic ______________________ favourable ______________________

feeble ______________________ tragic ______________________

strange ______________________ glorious ______________________

8 Add a **clause** to each line below.

When planning a narrative, ______________________.

If you are writing a first-person narrative, ______________________.

Write a flashback ______________________.

Add a flow diagram ______________________.

9 Complete each sentence with an **article** (*a, an* or *the*).

We are taking ______ trip to the Whitsundays.

______ school concert has been cancelled.

Do you know ______ answer to question 5?

May I have ______ ice-cream cone?

10 Circle the **simile**. Underline **word associations** for whole or parts of deciduous trees.

Deciduous trees lose their leaves each autumn. In Australia, the only winter deciduous tree is the Deciduous Beech. It grows to two metres tall. It has gnarled, twisted branches. Its leaves are shaped like crinkle-cut potato chips and they change from red to gold before they fall.

11 Rewrite the sentences with correct punctuation.

stop yelled felix from the side of the road

____

ms evanko is taking year 6 to the queensland art gallery on wednesday

____

last sunday artura saw torres strait islander canoes paddles baskets and pottery

____

12 Complete each sentence with one or more **phrases** that tell time (when).

They stopped searching ______________________.

______________________ they finished building the cubbyhouse.

The weary travellers arrived home ______________________.

'The vet will see your rat ______________________,' said the receptionist.

13 Circle the **idiom** in the sentence below. What does Otto mean?

'You're pulling my leg,' replied Otto after Arthur had finished telling his news.

____

____

Unit 25 Degrees of formality, questions

These texts show how the writer varies his writing for different audiences.

Correspondence

Dear Mr Wilson,

My mother suggested that I write to let you know I have now enrolled at my new school. As you advised, it is very cold here. Thank you again for the beanie. It is very colourful and warm. It will certainly be useful here in the snow. Please give my regards to my old class.

Yours sincerely,

Andreas De Luca

Hi Tony

Arrived here yesterday and we had heaps of fresh snow overnight. :-) We're going tobogganing today but I am not wearing that awful beanie Mr Wilson gave me. LOL Mum says it'd make a good tea-cosy (if she ever used a teapot). Dad says we should stick it on our letter box as a colourful beacon ;-). I'm going to donate it to a wildlife charity to use for keeping orphaned wombats warm. (I hope the colour scheme doesn't make them puke!) You will come and visit soon, won't you? Bye for now,

Andy

Rule The way writers or speakers address an audience shows the level of formality and social distance.

informal, friendly — *See you later, alligator.* — *Hey, everyone!*

formal, respectful — *Good evening, ladies and gentlemen.*

1 Read *Correspondence*. Circle the more formal form of address.

2 Circle the words that describe the relationship between Andreas and Mr Wilson.

formal	friendly	polite	distant	close
familiar	businesslike	informal	respectful	civil

3 Describe the relationship between Andreas and Tony.

---

4 Andreas shares two different opinions about the beanie with two different audiences. Summarise the opinions.

Opinion presented to Mr Wilson	Opinion presented to Tony

Grammar Rules! Student Book 6 (ISBN 9780655092544) © Tanya Gibb

5 Draw a line to link each situation with an appropriate form of address.

student speaker at a school	Dear Sir or Madam
letter to loved ones	Welcome, colleagues
text message to friend	Dear Mum and Dad
addressing conference delegates	:) hi how R U? I'll C U L8R.
business letter	To whom it may concern
letter to a government department	Good afternoon, fellow students

Tip

Questions can be open or closed.

Closed questions close down communication because they only need a short answer.

Which city did you like best?

Open questions open up communication. They require a more detailed response.

Why do you like novels by Sally Morgan?

6 Reword each **closed question** to Andreas as an **open question**.

Do you like the beanie Mr Wilson gave you?

___

Do you like your new school?

___

Do you like snow?

___

Tip

Questions are sometimes formed by adding a **question tag** to the end of a **statement** or **command**.

'That's all I have to get.' → *'That's all I have to get, isn't it?'*

7 Underline the **question tag** in *Correspondence*.

8 Add a **question tag** to each **statement** or **command**.

We should go home now ___

We'll drive there ___

She's running late ___

Jarrod and Yuka have finished with the computer ___

Tomohiro said he'd be here by 10 pm ___

Try it yourself!

Write an email to your principal **responding** to something in your school. Write another email to a friend or family member about the same topic. The emails should differ in formality and in the way you represent the topic to each audience. Discuss with a peer how language varies according to the audience.

Unit **26** Metaphor, alliteration, word associations

This **persuasive text** is a **menu** for a restaurant. It describes food items in ways that persuade readers to choose them.

The Melting Pot

DESTINATION: GASTRONOMIC!

French Crepes

A delicious blend of four vegan cheeses in a herbed cream sauce, wrapped in soft French crepes and baked until golden brown.

Mexican No-Beef Burritos

Tasty strips of plant-based beef with garlic and Mexican chilli beans, rolled in tortillas then topped with sour cream.

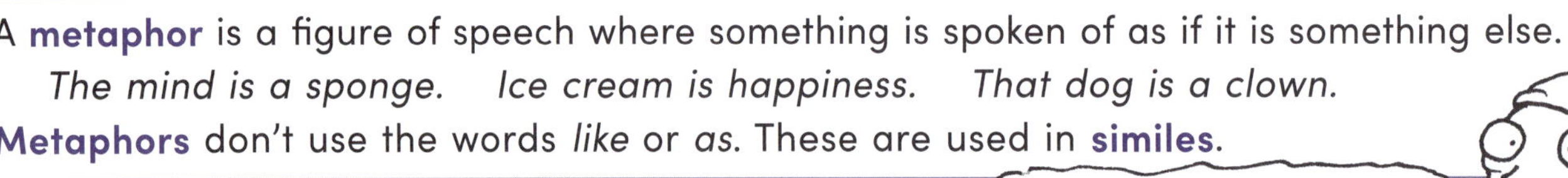

Moroccan Lamb

Delightful, tangy North African spices with the sweet flavours of sultanas and brown sugar complement sautéed vegetables served on a bed of couscous.

For descriptions of these other menu items, ask the waitstaff.

Scrumptious Greek souvlaki; chilled and refreshing beetroot and sour cream Russian borscht; succulent Japanese tempura; mouth-watering Thai-style coconut rice.

Tip A **metaphor** is a figure of speech where something is spoken of as if it is something else.
The mind is a sponge. *Ice cream is happiness.* *That dog is a clown.*
Metaphors don't use the words *like* or *as*. These are used in **similes**.

mmmMetaphor

1 Read *The Melting Pot.* Explain the **metaphor** in the title.

____

____

2 Complete each line to create **metaphors** of your own.

My heart is ______________________________

The sea leopard is ______________________________

The snow is ______________________________

In the dark bedroom, discarded clothing is ______________________________

The human brain is ______________________________

3 In *The Melting Pot,* circle the words for the places of origin of the foods.

4 In *The Melting Pot,* underline the **subjective** words that tell readers the food is delicious. Write five **synonyms** of your own for *delicious.* ______________________________

____

5 Write the **verbs** used in *The Melting Pot.* Then write five cooking **verbs** of your own.

____

____

Grammar Rules! Student Book 6 (ISBN 9780655092544) © Tanya Gibb

6 Write an example of **alliteration** used in *The Melting Pot*.

____

____

Tip Remember the tip on page 46.

7 Complete the table. Write the **proper noun** that refers to the people from each country. Then think of a type of food from each country. Use **noun groups** to label and describe foods. Add a bush tucker menu item in the top row.

Country (proper noun)	People (proper noun)	Food (noun group)
Australia		
Italy		
Spain		
Germany		
India		
Indonesia		
China		
Philippines		

8 Add a menu item of your own to *The Melting Pot*. Follow the pattern of the menu. Label and describe your menu item. Include how it is cooked and what it is served with.

____

____

____

9 Create **metaphors** for the human body.

hair: *limp strands of seaweed; soft wisps of fern; spikey echidna quills*

eyes ____

mouth ____

bloodstream ____

fingers ____

legs ____

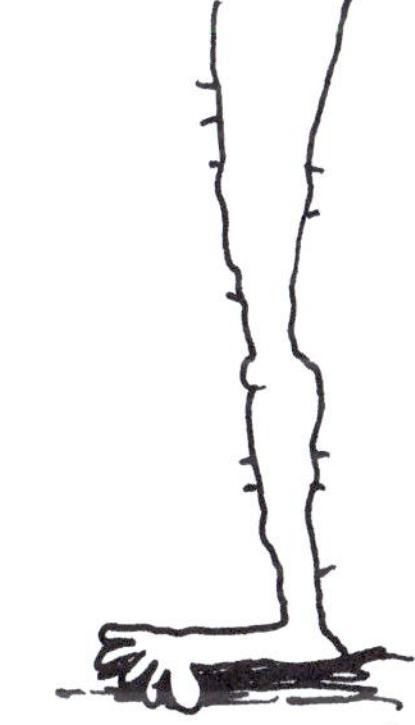

10 Use **alliteration** and **metaphors** to write descriptions of two people or places of your choice.

____

____

Design and create a menu for a restaurant of your own. Consider how to use descriptions to **persuade** your customers to want to eat your food. Use language that appeals to the senses: taste, sight, sound, smell and touch (how the food feels in your mouth).

Unit 27

Subject-verb agreement, proverbs, acronyms

The Rights of the Child

Host: We begin today by acknowledging the Traditional Custodians of this land known as Australia and pay respect to the Elders, past and present. Listeners, I'd like to introduce rap star DEEdee Kinks, who has just declared himself a campaigner for children's rights. What can you tell us about your work, DEEdee?

DEEdee: Yes, look, basically I'm using my fame and notoriety to publicise the fact that too many children around the world live under terrible conditions. Way back in 1948, the General Assembly of the United Nations proclaimed *The Universal Declaration of Human Rights* to advocate for the rights of all people of all ages, races, religions, genders and economic status. These rights included the rights of children. I believe we all share a global responsibility to promote the rights of children everywhere. As my momma always says: 'Where there's a will, there's a way', and another thing she always says is: 'Don't sit on the fence, Darryl'.

Host: Well, DEEdee, you are not just a pretty face!

This text is a podcast transcript. It includes **emotive vocabulary** to present a point of view and influence the audience to accept that point of view.

1 Read *The Rights of the Child*. Underline the **open question** asked by the host.

2 What does DEEdee hope to achieve by participating in the interview?

____

____

3 Write the **emotive words** and **phrases** used in *The Rights of the Child*.

____

____

Remember the tip on page 27.

An **acronym** is a word made up of the initial letters of other words.
UNICEF → **U**nited **N**ations **I**nternational **C**hildren's **E**mergency **F**und

4 Find out what these **acronyms** stand for.

QANTAS ____

PIN ____

ASAP ____

NAIDOC ____

UNHCR ____

WHO ____

Grammar Rules! Student Book 6 (ISBN 9780655092544) © Tanya Gibb

Tip

Proverbs are sayings that have a moral or a message.

Many hands make light work.

This proverb means: if a lot of people pitch in and help, things get done faster and easier.

5 Write the two **proverbs** used by DEEdee's mother. Write what each one means.

____

____

____

____

6 Write the meaning for these two other **proverbs** that DEEdee's mother liked to quote to him.

Actions speak louder than words.

____

Strike while the iron's hot.

____

7 What did the podcast host (interviewer) mean by saying DEEdee was *not just a pretty face?*

____

A **verb** must agree in number with its **subject**.

A **plural noun** needs a matching **verb**.	*The apples were eaten.*
A **singular noun** needs a matching **verb**.	*The apple was eaten.*
Collective nouns are singular.	*The orchard is thriving.*

8 Cross out the incorrect **verbs** in the brackets.

DEEdee: I now try to (makes / make) people aware of the work of UNICEF. In case listeners (is / are) not aware, UNICEF (are / is) an organisation that helps children all over the world. Quality of life (are / is) a child's right rather than a privilege. Children (is / are) precious.

9 Circle the **verb** that agrees with the **subject** in each sentence.

DEEdee's mother (is / are) influential in his life.

The band (is / are) on a world tour.

Interviewers (is / are) good at asking open questions.

DEEdee (was / were) a choir singer in primary school.

Write a **persuasive** text about a topic that interests you. Create a character, like DEEdee or an expert, to present the main arguments and supporting information. Work with a partner to record the radio interview using audio recording and editing equipment and music to enhance the recording.

Unit **28** Verb groups, subjective language

This persuasive text is a **discussion**. It uses **subjective language** to present two different points of view on a topic. It includes the writer's opinion.

There are two incredible natural wonders in the world that are so vast they can be seen from outer space. They are the Great Barrier Reef off the coast of Queensland, Australia, and the Grand Canyon in the United States of America. Which of these is the most spectacular?

Many people believe the Great Barrier Reef is the best natural wonder. At 2300 kilometres in length, it is the world's largest coral reef system. Colonies of tiny coral polyps have built the reef over thousands of years. It is truly a miracle of nature.

Other people think that the Grand Canyon deserves the title of best natural wonder in the world. The Colorado River has carved out the canyon over two billion years. The canyon is around 445 kilometres long and 1800 metres deep at its deepest point – that's almost two kilometres!

Both these wonders were created by nature and continue to evolve, but in my opinion, the Great Barrier Reef is a truly beautiful and precious part of this planet, and it gets my vote for best natural wonder of the world.

1 Read *Top Wonder.* What is the purpose of each paragraph?

Paragraph 1	Paragraph 2	Paragraph 3	Paragraph 4

2 Underline the phrases in *Top Wonder* that link the arguments.

3 Circle the **relating verbs** in *Top Wonder*. Hint! Don't confuse them with **auxiliary verbs**.

Remember the tip on page 37.

4 Write the two **thinking verbs** used to present opinions and judgements in *Top Wonder*.

______________________ ______________________

5 Write six other **thinking verbs** that could be used in a discussion to present an opinion.

____

6 Write the **verb group** used for the action of the polyps in *Top Wonder*. ______________________

7 Write the **verb group** used for the action of the river on the canyon. ______________________

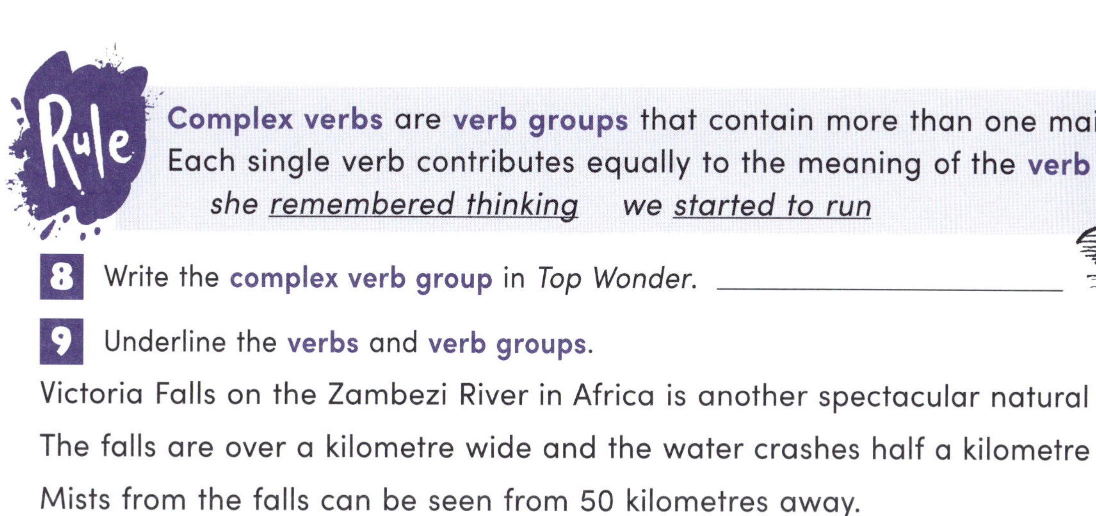

Complex verbs are **verb groups** that contain more than one main verb. Each single verb contributes equally to the meaning of the **verb group**.

she remembered thinking *we started to run*

8 Write the **complex verb group** in *Top Wonder*. ____________________

9 Underline the **verbs** and **verb groups**.

Victoria Falls on the Zambezi River in Africa is another spectacular natural wonder of the world. The falls are over a kilometre wide and the water crashes half a kilometre into the gorge below. Mists from the falls can be seen from 50 kilometres away.

Evaluative language is language that tells us people's opinions and judgements about something. **Subjective language** is evaluative. It tells the speaker or writer's opinion and judgement about something.

amazing scenery *a worthy cause* *a logical argument*

10 What **subjective language** used by the writer of *Top Wonder* shows that he or she values the two natural wonders discussed?

____

11 Use **evaluative language** to write opposite opinions to those below.

a useful app ____________________

an entertaining advertisement ______________________________

12 Write your opinion about a place in your local community being promoted as a tourist attraction. Use **subjective language**. (You might like to write in a tongue-in-cheek style.)

Write a sentence to introduce the area.

____

Present an argument in favour of it becoming a tourist attraction.

On the one hand, ____

____

Present an argument against it becoming a tourist attraction.

On the other hand, ____

____

Summarise your point of view.

In conclusion ____

____

Work with classmates to prepare a **discussion** as a digital text on a topic that interests the group. Use audio, video, images and graphics to present group members' differing opinions to a specific audience such as classmates or parents. Use **subjective** and **emotive language** to engage your audience.

Unit 29 Emotive vocabulary, subjective language, clauses

This text is **informative**. The author's point of view is evident in the **subjective language**.

RESISTANCE

Australia's First Peoples have a different history to tell from the history most Australians know about.

The First Nations history of Australia tells of the invasion of lands the people had lived on for tens of thousands of years. It tells of them being deprived of their agricultural and aquacultural grounds and access to resources and sacred sites.

The First Nations history of Australia includes accounts of the bravery and resilience of Aboriginal and Torres Strait Islander Peoples, including resistance heroes such as Pemulwuy, Truganini, Windradyne and Dundalli.

The First Nations history tells of Frontier Wars and brave warriors using guerrilla tactics to resist the invasion – small bands using stealth, mobility and surprise to attack the invaders who had superior numbers and weaponry. And First Nations history tells of hundreds of massacres of innocent First Nations women, children and elderly people.

1 Read *Resistance*. What do the following terms mean as used in *Resistance*? Use a dictionary.

invasion ______________________________

guerrilla ______________________________

agricultural grounds ______________________________

aquacultural grounds ______________________________

massacre ______________________________

2 What is the **main idea** in *Resistance*? Hint! The main idea is the idea the creator of the text wants you to accept.

____

3 Add a **main (independent) clause** to complete each sentence.

When people fight for their homeland, ______________________________.

After arriving in Australia in 1780, ______________________________.

If the first Australians were deprived of access to resources, ______________________________.

Although it was declared terra nullius, ______________________________.

Since it was declared terra nullius, ______________________________.

4 Circle **emotive** words and phrases in *Resistance*.

____

Grammar Rules! Student Book 6 (ISBN 9780655092544) © Tanya Gibb

Some words can function as **relating verbs** or **helping (auxiliary) verbs**.

is *are* *have*

A word is a **helping (auxiliary) verb** when it comes before another **verb** or **verb group**.

helping (auxiliary) verb *He <u>is</u> going out.*

relating verb *She <u>is</u> happy.*

5 Write whether each underlined word is a **relating verb** or a **helping (auxiliary) verb**.

Australia <u>was</u> declared terra nullius. ____________________

There <u>are</u> at least 274 islands in the Torres Strait. ____________________

Australia <u>was</u> colonised by the British in 1788. ____________________

Yumplatok <u>is</u> the most commonly spoken language in the Torres Strait Islands. ____________________

AIATSIS says there <u>are</u> more than 250 Indigenous languages in Australia. ____________________

A **dependent clause** can be **embedded** in a main clause. Commas sometimes separate the dependent clause within the **main clause**.

Truganini, <u>who was a Palawa person</u>, is often referred to as the last Tasmanian.

A comma separates a dependent clause from a **main (independent) clause** if the dependent clause comes first in the sentence.

<u>Although she resisted the invaders</u>, Truganini was eventually defeated.

6 Underline the **embedded clause** in each sentence.

My Uncle, who lives in Ipswich, has a massive mango tree in his yard.

This book about birds, which my friend gave me, is very useful.

Some libraries, which are trying to revive lost languages, have useful websites.

The possum that lives in Clint's mango tree has had a baby.

The cake that I saw Dad making was a banana cake.

7 Circle the **verb groups**. Underline the **dependent clauses** below.

The Latin phrase *res nullius* means 'nobody's thing'. In Roman times, wild animals or abandoned buildings were *res nullius* so anyone could seize them. *Res nullius* is the basis for the term *terra nullius*, which means 'nobody's land'. The British used the term *terra nullius* when seizing land from the Traditional Owners without compensation or treaty. *Terra nullius* was overturned in the High Court of Australia in 1992 when the court recognised Traditional Owners' claims on land through native title.

Research an influential or celebrated First Nations Australian, such as Mandawuy Yunupingu, Faith Bandler, Mum Shirl (Shirley Colleen Smith), Oodgeroo Noonuccal, Neville Bonner, Eleanor Harding, Vincent Lingiari, Albert Namatjira, Bronwyn Bancroft or Charles Perkins. Create a **biography** to present to the class.

Unit 30 Revision

1 Add a **question tag** to each statement.

You need a haircut, ______________________

Ruby is not coming, ______________________

Yoko's finished picking flowers, ______________________

It's a long drive to Mparntwe, ______________________

You know that Mparntwe is Alice Springs, ______________________

2 Complete each line to create **metaphors**.

A daffodil is ______________________

My headache is ______________________

School students are ______________________

My school bag is ______________________

3 Write a list of **synonyms** and **antonyms** that could be used in a poem for a place of your choice.

____

____

4 Underline the **main (independent) clause** in each sentence below. Hint! Look out for **conjunctions** and for **dependent clauses** that are embedded in the main clause.

Our guide Kirili, who is a Arakwal Bundjalung woman, was passionate about sharing her knowledge of Country.

In Australian English, a slang word for hard work is 'yakka', which comes from the Yuggera word 'yaga'.

Dad had a photo of Jonny when he was a nipper.

Since Molly moved out, the old house has become derelict.

You'd better report the dog if you think it's lost.

You can search for poems that have been written by First Nations authors on the internet.

5 Choose the correct **verb** in brackets to match the **singular** and **plural subjects**.

The group (is / are) on tour.

Canada's flag (is / are) red and white.

Parents (is / are) influential in every family.

Jai and Kuda (is / are) cousins.

Children (was / were) allowed in for free.

6 Write whether the underlined verb is a **relating verb** or a **helping (auxilary) verb**.

Rats <u>make</u> great pets. ______________________

We <u>have</u> a pet ferret. ______________________

Global warming <u>is</u> a worry. ______________________

Tourists <u>are</u> showing greater environmental awareness. ______________________

Grammar Rules! Student Book 6 (ISBN 9780655092544) © Tanya Gibb

7 Draw a line to connect each **proverb** to its meaning.

Look before you leap.	People get in each other's way if they try to do the same thing at the same time.
Too many cooks spoil the broth.	Don't count on things that haven't happened yet.
Every cloud has a silver lining.	Don't delay action.
Never put off till tomorrow what you can do today.	Try to look on the bright side of every situation.
Don't count your chickens until they hatch.	Think about what you are doing before you do it.

8 Join the **simple sentences** to create one **complex sentence**.

David Unaipon's image is on the fifty dollar note. He was a Ngarrindjeri man. He was an inventor and author.

____

____

9 Rewrite each sentence as **quoted speech**.

The tourists claimed that they had seen polar bears in Churchill.

____

Kirra found out that black bears eat berries.

____

The hikers said that they always eat porridge before a hike.

____

Chi asked Hannah if she knew that koalas were not bears.

____

10 Circle the **subjective** words and phrases that tell the writer's opinions.

Stunt Morons

Throughout history, brave (or stupid) people have made attempts to conquer Niagara Falls. In 1901, a woman called Annie Taylor became the first person to survive a trip over the falls. She must have been nuts to go over Niagara Falls in a wooden barrel, but she made history. In 1911, Bobby Leach broke both knees and a jaw going over the falls in a steel barrel. He would have suffered badly because medicine wasn't what it is now. He probably never healed properly. Other foolhardy individuals have succeeded or died over the years. Why anyone would want to even try it is beyond me.

11 Write an **evaluation** of Annie Taylor's trip over Niagara Falls that makes positive judgements.

____

____

Chichén Itzá

This **informative** text is the transcript of a television interview. It uses technical terms for aspects of the topic and **pronouns** for reference.

Compere: Situated in the jungles of the Yucatán peninsula in Mexico are the ruins of Chichén Itzá.
These ruins are classified as one of the seven wonders of the world.
Chichén Itzá was once a great temple of the Mayan civilisation.
This evening we welcome Professor Lee Rodriguez to the program.
Professor Rodriguez is currently working with archaeologists at the Chichén Itzá site. Professor, tell us about your work.

Professor Rodriguez: Yes, certainly. The Mayans lived at Chichén Itzá from the sixth to the fifteenth centuries. I'll tell you this: they were great astronomers, writers and architects, but they were also very religious. They believed in a great many gods and they believed those gods wanted regular human sacrifices. For example, we have discovered evidence of a ball game called pok-ta-pok. This was played in a great courtyard at Chichén Itzá, and on ceremonial occasions, the losers of the game were sacrificed to placate the gods.

Compere: Arrghh! How horrific!

Professor Rodriguez: Yes. The Mayans also sacrificed prisoners, slaves and orphaned children.

1 Does the professor use **evaluative language**? Explain.

____

____

2 Who does the **personal pronoun** *we* refer to in *Chichén Itzá*? ______________

Who does the **personal pronoun** *they* refer to? ______________

Demonstrative pronouns replace **nouns**.

this *that* *these* *those* *This is my bus.*

In the **noun group**, *this, that, these* and *those* are **determiners**.
They are used to point out. *This bus is mine.*

3 Write the **noun groups** from the text that include words that point out (*this, that, these, those*).

____

In spoken language, gestures often help to make meaning clear when **demonstrative pronouns** are used.
'Get that!'

Grammar Rules! Student Book 6 (ISBN 9780655092544) © Tanya Gibb

4 Create a cartoon for each fact. Use **demonstrative pronouns** in speech bubbles.

At Chichén Itzá, Mayans stuffed dead people's mouths with food before burying them under the floors of their homes.

The Mayans at Chichén Itzá valued crossed eyes as a symbol of beauty.

Losers at pok-ta-pok were sacrificed.

Tip **Demonstrative pronouns** can refer to a word that came before the demonstrative pronoun or will come after it.

5 Complete each line. Write what the **demonstrative pronoun** is referring to.

Listen to this. ______________________________.

This is what I have to say. ______________________________.

______________________________. Now that I have told you this, I feel much better.

6 Find a **demonstrative pronoun** in *Chichén Itzá* that comes before the speech it refers to. Write the sentences.

____

7 Use the words in the box to complete the sentences. Use capitals where necessary.

it	this	she	that	her

Professor Rodriguez trained in Mexico. __________ spent five years at university. After __________, she focused on Mayan culture. She said __________ is what she enjoys most. Mayan culture fascinated __________ and __________ still does.

Try it yourself! Write an **information report** about something you are learning in class. Then work with a partner to role-play your text as a television interview. Perform your interview for the class.

Unit 32

Personification, imagery, homophones, prefixes

This **persuasive** text is a travel advertisement. It uses **personification** to make the landscape seem alive so that readers will want to go there.

Lion Safari, Kenya

Begin with the knowledge that an African lion safari is like no other travel destination.

Wake to the fervent call of the wild.

Sigh at shifting herds of antelope, wildebeest, zebra, hippopotamus and elephant.

Breathe in the immensity of the grassy plains.

Sense the pride as a family of lions relaxes in the sun.

Experience the stalking of the lion as it stalks its prey.

Observe the king as he observes his kingdom from a rocky throne.

Listen as night descends, conveying safety and danger.

Sleep to the lulling sounds of the untamed.

Africa – no place like it in the end.

Visit Kenya. Call 1800 888 810.

Rule

Personification means giving human qualities to non-human things.

The mud sucked on my toes. *The trees stood guard at the entrance.*

1 Read *Lion Safari, Kenya*. Underline two examples of **personification**.

2 Draw a line to match each human quality to a non-human thing.

the television	raged angrily
sails of a yacht in a storm	smiled kindly
sunshine	screamed in terror
the shadows	waited malevolently in the dusk
night	played across my bedroom floor
the wind	looked back at me

3 Complete each line with a human quality to **personify** each thing.

the lightning ______________________

dry plains ______________________

night ______________________

the wind ______________________

the last piece of chocolate ______________________

Rule

Imagery is when language is used to appeal to the senses of readers and listeners and help them imagine what something is like.

4 Which of the human senses does *Lion Safari, Kenya* appeal to? Add an example of each from the text.

____

____

Grammar Rules! Student Book 6 (ISBN 9780655092544) © Tanya Gibb

5 Change each **verb** to a **noun**. Then use the **noun** in a sentence. Hint! To help you work out the **noun**, put *the* in front of it.

hoping ______________________________

observe ______________________________

believe ______________________________

performing ______________________________

Rule

A **homophone** is a word that sounds like another word but is spelt differently.
Some verbs and nouns form **homophone** pairs.
The noun is spelt with a *c*: *I have my licence.*
The verb is spelt with an *s*: *I am licensed.*

6 Change each word from a **verb** to a **noun**. Then use the **nouns** in a sentence.

prophesising ______________________________

practise ______________________________

7 Write the **verbs** used as commands in *Lion Safari, Kenya.*

____

8 Re-read *Lion Safari, Kenya.*

Find two pairs of **synonyms**.

____

Write four pairs of **antonyms**.

____

Find a **metaphor**.

____

Tip

Antonyms can be formed by adding a prefix or changing the prefix.
mis– *dis–* *un–* *in–* *ill–* *non–* *ir–* *anti–*
understood → *misunderstood* *rational* → *irrational* *increase* → *decrease*

9 Find two words in *Lion Safari, Kenya* that have **antonyms** formed by prefixes.

____

Try it yourself!

Choose a holiday destination. Write a poetry-style advertisement that uses **imagery** and **personification** to appeal to the senses to make a reader want to visit there. Publish your advertisement.

Unit 33

First- and third- person narrators, characters, plot

These three texts have the same plot and characters. Text 1 uses a **third-person narrator**. Text 2 uses a **first-person narrator**. Text 3 is a play script.

Don't Let Them In

Text 1

They'd heard noises outside. Mum wouldn't be home for at least an hour. Nia crouched below the windowsill while her brother, Ethan, crept towards the front door. The doorknob slowly began to turn. They each held their breath, frozen on the spot, eyes glued to the doorknob.

Text 2

I lifted my head above the windowsill to peep beneath the curtain and out through the windowpane but I couldn't see anything. It was dark outside and none of our windows had a view of the front door anyway. I looked over at Ethan and shook my head to indicate I couldn't see anything, but we knew what was out there. Ethan was frozen on the spot, wide-eyed and terrified. Mum wouldn't be home for at least an hour.

Then the doorknob began to turn.

Text 3

IT IS NIGHT. TWO CHILDREN ARE HOME ALONE.

(stealthy, shuffling sounds heard offstage)

Nia: (crouching under the windowsill, holding finger to lips, whispers): Shhhhhhhhhh...

Ethan: (crawling to Nia, whispers) Can you see anything?

Nia: (mouthing) No.

Ethan: (whispers) What will we do?

1 Read *Don't Let Them In*. Write the events in Text 2 with a **first-person narrator** from Ethan's point of view. What might he be thinking and feeling? What will Ethan do next?

____

____

____

2 The **plot** in a narrative needs to have **tension** or **conflict** so that readers want to read on and find out what happens to the characters. What possibilities are there for tension and suspense in the plot of *Don't Let Them In*?

____

____

____

3 Which version of *Don't Let Them In* do you think is the most suspenseful: Text 1, 2 or 3? Why?

____

How does the author create the suspense? Do you want to read the rest of the narrative to find out who or what is outside? Explain. ______________________________

____

Grammar Rules! Student Book 6 (ISBN 9780655092544) © Tanya Gibb

4 What do you know about the characters of Nia and Ethan and their relationship so far in *Don't Let Them In?*

5 Write the next paragraph for Text 1 in *Don't Let Them In.*

6 In each text in *Don't Let Them In*, which character seems to be the main character? Explain your reasoning.

Text 1 ______

Text 2 ______

Text 3 ______

7 In Text 2, the narrator, Nia, says, *'we knew what was out there'.*
What do you think it could be?

Tip Remember that a **flashback** helps readers understand a character and the current situation in the plot.

8 Write a flashback for Text 1 *Don't Let Them In* that explains where the mother had gone.

They'd heard noises outside. Mum wouldn't be home for at least an hour. She'd warned them before she left ______

9 Write four words or phrases used in *Don't Let Them In* that contribute to the atmosphere in the texts.

Play scripts include information to set the scene as well as **stage directions** for the characters and instructions regarding how the **dialogue** should be spoken. Choose a section of dialogue from a novel you are reading and rework it as a play script. Or, write a narrative of your own as a play script for classmates to perform.

Unit 34

Word origins, prefixes and suffixes

This information report uses words from languages other than English to represent culturally diverse events and celebrations.

Multicultural Australia

Australia is a democracy. The term democracy comes from two Greek words: 'demos', which means 'the people', and 'kratos', which means 'rule'. So, 'democracy' means 'rule by the people', where the people vote for the government. In Australia, the term 'democracy' also means that everyone has equal rights.

More than twenty-five million people live in Australia. These twenty-five million people identify with more than 270 cultural backgrounds. The term 'Australian' is applied to all citizens of Australia whether they are born here or overseas, and regardless of ethnicity or cultural background.

This cultural diversity is celebrated through festivals and special events. Celebrations and festivals include Lunar New Year, Diwali (the Hindu Festival of Lights), Ramadan (a period of fasting in the Islamic calendar), Hanukkah (a Jewish festival), Christmas and Easter (two Christian festivals), and Vesak (a Buddhist festival), among many, many others.

Tip

Many words in English have their origins in other languages. Words are made up of their root as well as **suffixes** and **prefixes**.

dent (Latin base) = tooth; ist (suffix) = one who→dentist = one who works with teeth

Some words have been adopted directly from other languages.

spaghetti (Italian) *sushi (Japanese)*

1 Read *Multicultural Australia*. Underline the words that are from languages other than English.

2 The **suffix** *–less* means 'free from' or 'without'. Write the word in *Multicultural Australia* that has the **suffix** *–less*. ______________________

Write three other words of your choice that use the **suffix** *–less*.

____

Tip

Prefixes and **suffixes** affect the meaning of words.

The **prefix** *voco* is from the Latin *vocatum* meaning 'I call'.

3 These words are all derived from the Latin word *vocatum*. Write the definition of each word.

vocal ______________________

advocate ______________________

evoke ______________________

evocative ______________________

vocative ______________________

Grammar Rules! Student Book 6 (ISBN 9780655092544) © Tanya Gibb

4 *Celebrare* is from Latin. It means to assemble in large numbers to honour something or someone. Write the words in *Multicultural Australia* that are derived from *celebrare*.

_______________ _______________

5 Write three extra words that begin with *celebr–*.

____

6 Write three **compound nouns** used in *Multicultural Australia*.

____

7 Underline the **noun groups** in the sentences below.
Choose one of the sentences and make a poster to represent the words and meaning.

Hindu people celebrate Diwali, which is the Festival of Lights. They exchange gifts and sweets and celebrate the triumph of good over evil.

Lunar New Year is a particularly popular celebration in Australia. Lion dances, dragon dances and firecrackers are used symbolically to scare off evil spirits.

Vietnamese people celebrate Tet New Year with dragon dances and street decorations. Homes are decorated with fresh flowers and people cook special foods.

A very important festival for Buddhists is Vesak, or Buddha day. This festival celebrates the life, enlightenment and death of Buddha. People celebrate with candles, flowers and food.

Brackets are used around words that:
- add meaning or make meaning clearer *Diwali (the Hindu Festival of Lights)*
- give stage directions in a play script *Husny: (walks off stage) Goodbye, everyone.*
- provide reference information.

A complete sentence inside brackets has the punctuation inside the brackets too.

8 Add **brackets** where appropriate.

ANZAC Day the anniversary of the Gallipoli landing is commemorated on 25th April each year.

Passover a Jewish festival commemorates the passing over or sparing of the Hebrews from slavery in approximately 1300 BCE.

Wayne: enters stage right Hello, everyone. Stops centre stage.

Rosalea: follows Wayne and stands to his right Hi!

Research a particular festival or multicultural celebration and write an **information report** about it. Collect images to illustrate your information report. Collate reports from class members and create a digital presentation to present the information to the class.

Unit 35 Revision

1 Rewrite this sentence as **reported speech**.

'I enjoy travelling to amazing places,' said Sophia.

____

2 Rewrite this sentence so that it addresses the reader directly.

People need to remember to show respect for local customs when they are travelling.

____

3 Rewrite this sentence using **quoted speech**.

Anthony asked Tahlia to take his photo in front of the statue.

____

4 Complete the sentences with words from the box. Use capital letters where necessary.

the
these
this
those

__________ photos look terrific but __________ are out of focus.

'__________ travel brochure is about Italy,' said Juan.

'Can you pass __________ travel brochure on Italy?' asked Luigi.

5 Imagine what the underlined **demonstrative pronouns** refer to in each **sentence**. Write statements on the lines.

'______________________________________. Now that you know about <u>this</u> I feel much better,' said Tomas.

'Listen to <u>this</u>,' announced Carla. '______________________________________

______________________________________.'

6 Write a sentence that **personifies** each thing.

flower ______________________________________

sun ______________________________________

gorilla ______________________________________

spider ______________________________________

7 Write six **synonyms** for *said*.

____

8 Write four pairs of **antonyms** to represent how people feel about school holidays.

____

____

Grammar Rules! Student Book 6 (ISBN 9780655092544) © Tanya Gibb

9 Change each underlined **verb** into a **noun** and use the **noun** in a sentence.

We'll <u>celebrate</u> on Saturday.

___

Joel fondly <u>remembered</u> his trip to Bali.

___

It was very moving when John <u>read</u> his poem on stage.

___

10 Circle the **abstract nouns** in the box.

safety	highway	monorail	travel	excitement	effort	ticket	pleasure

11 Rewrite the **simple sentences** as one **complex sentence**.

Our town flooded last July. Some people lost everything in the floodwaters. Volunteers from the Sikh community came with food vans. They helped feed people.

___

___

___

12 Write three words with the **suffix** *–ship*.

___

13 Write five words with the **prefix** *mis–*.

___

14 Add **brackets** where they are needed.

In Australia, Father's Day a day honouring fathers is celebrated on the first Sunday in September.

Mother's Day a day honouring mothers is celebrated on the second Sunday in May each year.

Kyle: turns to face Flora Will you marry me?

Flora: claps hands together Yes!

15 Choose **connectives** from the box to complete the recount. Use capitals where appropriate.

after
finally
during
at first
once
when
until
while

___ the school holidays, I travelled to Canberra with my family. ___ we were there, we visited the Australian War Memorial. ___ I thought it was going to be really boring but ___ I had looked at the first exhibit I loved it. I was amazed ___ I saw dioramas of actual battles. We stayed ___ closing so that we could hear the piper play the Last Post. ___ we ___ left, I asked my parents if we could go back again the next day.

Glossary

Look at the page number in the circle to find more information about the rule or tip.

abbreviation......a short form of a word (29)

acronym.............a word made up of the initial letters of other words (60)

adjective............a word that tells more about a **noun**

adjectival phrase (10) *to classify* (10)
comparative and superlative (23) *to describe* (10)
for possession (17) *to quantify or tell number* (15)

adverb................a word that adds meaning to a **verb**, **adjective** or another adverb (13)

can tell place (where) or manner (how) (13)
can tell time (when) (9) *modal adverbs* (39)

alliteration.........when the beginnings of words have the same sounds (46)

antonyms...........words with opposite meanings (49)

apostrophe........in contractions (29) for possession (45)

article.................(*a, an, the*) used in front of a **noun** or at the beginning of a **noun group** (22) (49)

clause.................a unit of meaning that includes a **verb**

adjectival clause, adverbial clause (36) *dependent clause* (12) (36)
embedded (dependent) clause (65) *main (independent) clause* (12)

cohesion............how a text holds together including through using **pronouns**, **connectives** or **word associations** (32) (49)

comma...............a punctuation mark that separates:

a dependent clause from a main clause (65)
quoted speech (25)

conjunction.......a word that connects clauses in a sentence (9)

connective.........a word or words that link ideas in a text through reason, addition, time or comparison (34)

contraction........when two words are joined to shorten them and an apostrophe replaces the letter/s left out (29)

determiners.......words (including articles) that identify or point out (22)

emotive vocabulary..words and phrases used to elicit an emotional response from readers/viewers/listeners (27) (38)

evaluative language.........language that shows the speaker's/writer's judgement (63)

flashback...........a literary device that authors use to tell readers about something that happened before the story commenced (53)

first-person narrative....a story told by one of the characters using *I, me, we* or *us* (53)

formal/informal language............how language varies in formality according to the situation and audience (28) (56)

homophone........a word that sounds like another word but is spelt differently 71

idiom..................an expression that is understood but means something different from the literal meaning of the words 20 28

imagery..............language used to appeal to the senses 70

informal language...see *formal language*

metaphor...........figurative language where one thing is said to be another 56

noun....................a naming word for people, places, animals, things and ideas 10

abstract 21 *collective* 45 *noun group* 10

objective language...language that is factual and unbiased 11 44

parody................when a known or familiar text is imitated to create humour 46

personification..........when human qualities are given to non-human things 70

possessive apostrophe....a punctuation mark used to show possession 45

prefix..................letters or a word part added to the beginning of a word to change its meaning 74

prepositional phrase................a group of words that consist of a **preposition** followed by a **noun** or **pronoun**; tells place (where), time (when) and manner (with whom, what or how) 14

can modify a noun (adjectival phrase) 10

pronoun.............a word that refers to or replaces a **noun** 14

demonstrative 68 *personal* 16 *possessive* 17 *relative* 35

proverb..............a well-known saying or expression that offers wisdom or advice 20 61

question............a sentence that asks for information or an opinion 57

quoted (direct) speech....the actual speech someone said, shown in quotation marks 25

reported (indirect) speech.....speech that is reported and not directly quoted 26

sentence............a group of words that makes sense and includes at least one **verb** 12

complex sentence 12 35 *compound sentence* 12

simple sentence 12 *sentence opener* 32

simile..................when something is compared to something else using *like* or *as* 9

subjective language....words and phrases that show a point of view, opinion or bias 11 42

suffix..................a letter/letters added to the end of words 21 74

synonym............words that have similar meanings 27

third-person narrative......a story told by someone outside the narrative 57

verb....................a doing (action), being (relating), saying or feeling word 8

agreement with a noun (subject) 61 *auxiliary (helping)* 8 24 65

modal verbs 24 39 *relating (being)* 37 65 *tense* 8 24

verb group 8 24 63

word associations.words used as reference in texts to help with textual **cohesion** 33 49

word base.........the root or stem of a word to which affixes are added 74